CHRONICLES OF CHICORA WOOD

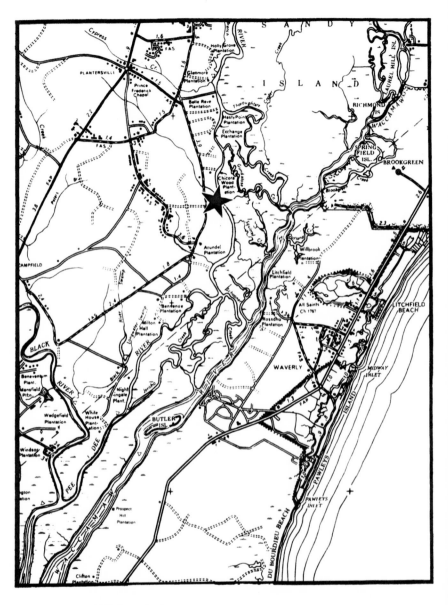

THE WACCAMAW NECK AND ITS PLANTATIONS

CHRONICLES OF "CHICORA WOOD"

ELIZABETH W. ALLSTON PRINGLE
AUTHOR OF "A WOMAN RICE PLANTER"

ILLUSTRATED

ATLANTA
CHEROKEE PUBLISHING COMPANY

Copyright Renewed 1950

By B. Allston Moore

Reprinted in 1976 by Cherokee Publishing Company through an arrangement with the Copyright owner, Benjamin Allston Moore of Charleston, nephew of the author.

Pringle, Elizabeth   Waties Allston, 1845-1921.
    Chronicles of Chicora Wood / by Elizabeth W. Allston Pringle. — Atlanta : Cherokee Pub. Co., 1976, c1922.
    viii, 369 p., [2] leaves of plates : ill. ; 23 cm.
    Includes index.
    ISBN 0-87797-036-X : $10.00

        1. Pringle, Elizabeth Waties Allston, 1845-1921.   2. Charleston, S.C.--Social life and customs.   3. Chicora Wood, S.C.   4. Charleston, S.C.—Biography. 5. Plantation life—South Carolina.   I. Title.
F279.C453P74   1976   975.7'915'030924   76-5346
                               [B]   MARC

Library of Congress   76

PRINTED IN THE UNITED STATES OF AMERICA
ISBN: 978-0-87797-036-1 Hardcover
ISBN: 978-0-87797-365-2 Paper

Cherokee Publishing Company
P O Box 1730, Marietta, GA 30061

PREFACE

As I sit in the broad piazza, watching the closing of the day, I gaze into the vistas of moss-draped giant oaks. All is mystery, the mystery of nature, the mystery of the ages. These oaks, still strong, still beautiful, have seen generations pass. Through their filmy vistas the god of the day is sending his gleaming shafts as he has always done.

But brighter to me than these last rays is the pageant of the Past, which sweeps before me now: scenes as intense as the flaming sky, incidents as tender as the fleecy clouds, years as dark and tragic as that leaden storm-bank at the horizon's edge, but redeemed from utter despair by a courage and a sacrifice equal in splendor to its illumined summits.

In my memory are stored the beauty and pathos of these years. Shall I let all this die without a word? These pictures I have treasured — so full of beauty and color — shall I let them fade, even as the sunset, into gray oblivion? I cannot bring before you as clearly as I would the charm and glamour of the past, but I can at least give a faint idea of "the days that are no more."

CONTENTS

PART I—MY FATHER

CHAPTER   PAGE

I. Origin of the Two L Allstons . . 3

II. Planter and Citizen 12

III. My Brother's Narrative . . . 26

PART II—MY MOTHER

IV. Early Days and Old Field School 43

V. Daddy Tom and Daddy Prince — Death of Little Mother So Beloved 53

VI. Marriage 57

VII. Move to Canaan — Aunt Blythe . 67

VIII. First Child — Plantation Life . 81

IX. First Grieving 94

PART III—MYSELF

X. Baby Woes 107

XI. The Little Schoolhouse — Boarding-School 123

XII. Summer on the Sea — School and Della's Illness and Trip Abroad — Papa Elected Governor . . 137

XIII. Christmas at Chicora Wood . . 150

XIV. Life in Charleston — Preparations for War 160

XV. Boarding-School in War Times . 176

CONTENTS

PART IV — WAR TIMES

CHAPTER   PAGE

XVI. THE WEDDING 187

XVII. CROWLEY HILL — OUR PLACE OF REFUGE DURING THE WAR . . . 192

XVIII. SORROW 200

XIX. LOCH ADÈLE 213

XX. SHADOWS 218

XXI. PREPARING TO MEET SHERMAN . . 221

XXII. THEY COME! 229

XXIII. DADDY HAMEDY'S APPEAL — IN THE TRACK OF SHERMAN'S ARMY . . 239

XXIV. SHADOWS DEEPEN 248

XXV. GLEAMS OF LIGHT 250

XXVI. TAKING THE OATH 260

PART V — READJUSTMENT

XXVII. GLEAMS OF LIGHT FROM MY DIARY 283

XXVIII. AUNT PETIGRU — MY FIRST GERMAN 298

XXIX. MAMMA'S SCHOOL 307

XXX. THE SCHOOL A SUCCESS 316

XXXI. 1868 331

XXXII. CHICORA WOOD 340

XXXIII. DADDY ANCRUM'S STORY 349

ILLUSTRATIONS

Chicora Wood . . . . Front Dust Jacket

The Waccamaw Neck and Its Plantations . . . Frontispiece

Mrs. Benjamin Allston (née Charlotte Anne Allston),
Mother of R. F. W. Allston 175A
Miniature by Fraser

Mr. and Mrs. R. F. W. Allston (née Adèle Petigru) . 175B
Portraits by Flagg about 1850

Mrs. William Allston (née Ester La Brosse de
Mahboeuf) 175A

Adèle Allston at Sixteen 212A

James Louis Petigru 212A
Miniature by Fraser

Mrs. Pringle at Chicora Wood 212B

PART I
MY FATHER

CHAPTER I

ORIGIN OF THE TWO L ALLSTONS

JOHN ALLSTON, of St. John's, Berkeley, was born in England in 1666, and came to this country between 1685 and 1694. He was descended from the ancient family of Allstone, through John Allston, of Saxham Hall, Newton, Suffolk, which was the seat of the Allstons for several hundred years. An Allston was the Saxon Lord of Stanford in Norfolk before the Conquest, and was dispossessed by the Normans. The old Saxon names of Rath Alstan, Alstane, were but variants of the name which John of St. John's spelled Alstane, until the signature of his will (1718), when he wrote it Allston. The motto was "Immotus," * " Az. ten stars, crest an estoile in a crescent argent."

John Allston, of St. John's, Berkeley, had a number of children, as self-respecting people of that date usually had, but we are concerned only with the descendants of his eldest son, John, who was the grandfather of Benjamin Allston, my father's father, and those of his second son, William, who was the grandfather of Charlotte Ann

* See vol. 1, page Q119, *Encyclopedia Heraldica.*

[3]

Allston, my father's mother. So his parents were second cousins.

Ben Allston died when his second son, Robert, was only eight years old. The boy was educated at Mr. Waldo's school in Georgetown until he was sixteen, when his widowed mother determined to send him to West Point. He entered in 1817, graduating in June, 1821, this being the first class which made the four years' course under Colonel Sylvanus Thayer. He was appointed lieutenant in the 3d Artillery, and assigned to duty on the Coast Survey under Lieutenant-Colonel Kearney, of the Topographical Engineers. In this position he assisted in surveying the harbors of Plymouth and Provincetown, Mass., and the entrance to Mobile Bay. While on duty here he got letters from his mother telling of her difficulties, which demanded his immediate presence at home. He asked for leave of absence, but being refused this by his commanding officer, he resigned his commission February, 1822, bought a horse and rode through northern Alabama and Georgia, then inhabited by Indians, to Charleston, and thence to Georgetown, S. C.

His mother's difficulties in managing her property of landed estate and negroes had been great,

[4]

and added to this was the effort of the purchaser of a plantation adjoining Chicora on the south to seize a tract of land (attempting to prove that this land belonged to his plantation), which when cleared became four of her best rice-fields. This had kept her in constant fiery correspondence, until my father felt it his duty to resign and come home and settle the matter.

He employed the lawyer of greatest repute at the moment, James L. Petigru; the case was brought into court, and my grandmother's title to the land established beyond question. She did not long survive to enjoy having her son at home to take the burden of the management of her affairs, for she died October 24, 1824, after a short illness of pleurisy, in her fifty-fourth year. This was a very great sorrow to my father, for he had for her an intense affection with a sense of protection. She was beautiful and very small, so that the servants always spoke of her as "Little Miss" in distinction to Aunt Blythe, who was "Big Miss." According to the custom of the day, the land was all left to the sons, charged with legacies to the daughters, so my father's patrimony consisted of large tracts of swamp land in Georgetown and Marion and seventeen negroes, subject to a debt to his sisters which amounted to more than the value of the property. He entered upon its management with great energy, surveyed the land himself, cleared and drained the swamps and converted them into valuable rice-fields.

In this work his military education was of great service to him. In 1823 he was elected surveyor-general of the State, an office which he held for four years. In 1828 he was returned by the people of Winyah to the lower house of the legislature, and in 1832 was returned to the Senate. About this time he attained the rank of colonel of the militia, service of the State. He continued to be returned to the Senate, and was president of that body from 1850 to 1856, when he was elected governor. But I must go back. During the lawsuit about the land my father was entertained by James L. Petigru, came to know the lawyer's sister, Adèle Petigru, and fell in love with her; and she finally yielded to his suit, and they were married in 1832 and went at once to his plantation, Chicora Wood, fourteen miles north of Georgetown, on the Great Pee Dee River.

I am always afraid of bursting out into praise of my father, for I adored him, and thought him the wisest and best man in the world, and still do think he was a most unusual mixture of firmness and gentleness, with rare executive ability. But I have always found, in reading biographies and sketches, that the unstinted and reiterated praises of the adoring writers rouses one's opposition, and I write this with the hope of bringing to his grandchildren the knowledge and appreciation of my father's character. I will try to draw his portrait with a few firm strokes, and leave the respect and admiration to be aroused by it. Now that slavery is a thing of the past, the younger generation in our Southland really know nothing about the actual working of it, and they should know to understand and see the past in its true light. Slavery was in many ways a terrible misfortune, but we know that in the ancient world it was universal, and no doubt the great Ruler of the world, "that great First Cause, least understood," allowed it to exist for some reason of His own.

The colony of North and South Carolina, then one, entreated the mother country to send no more slaves. "We want cattle, horses, sheep, swine, we don't want Africans." But the Africans continued to come. The Northeastern States were the first to get rid of the objectionable human property when conscientious scruples arose as to

the owning of slaves — in some instances by free-
ing them, but in many more instances by selling
them in the Southern States. There is no doubt
that in the colder climate slave labor was not
profitable. When the Civil War came, the Southern planters were reduced from wealth to poverty
by the seizure of their property which they held
under the then existing laws of the country. It
is a long and tangled story — and I do not pretend
to judge of its rights and wrongs. I have no
doubt that the Great Father's time for allowing
slavery was at an end. I myself am truly thankful that slavery is a thing of the past, and that I
did not have to take up the burden of the ownership of the one hundred people my father left me
in his will (all mentioned by name), with a pretty
rice-plantation called Exchange two miles north
of Chicora Wood. I much prefer to have had to
make my own living, as I have had to do, except
for the short six years of my married life, than to
have had to assume the care and responsibility of
those hundred negroes, soul and body. I have
had a happy life, in spite of great sorrow and continued work and strain, but I am quite sure that
with my sensitive temperament and fierce Hugue-
not conscience I never could have had a happy
life under the burden of that ownership.

It would have been a comfort, however, if we could have gathered up something from my father's large property, but we did not. Just before the war my mother's brother, Captain Tom Petigru, of the navy, died, leaving a childless widow. She lived in Charleston, in her beautiful home with large yard and garden, at the corner of Bull and Rutledge Streets, and was a rich woman, as riches were counted in those days — owning a large farm in Abbeville County, where the Giberts and Petigrus had originally settled, and also a rice-plantation, "Pipe Down," on Sandy Island on the Waccamaw, not far from my father's estates, also one hundred negroes. As soon as Uncle Tom died, Aunt Ann wrote to my father, asking him as a great favor to buy her plantation and negroes, as she felt quite unequal to the management and care of them. My father replied immediately that it was impossible for him to comply with her request, that he had his hands full managing his own property, and that he specially felt he had already more negroes than he desired. Aunt Ann continued her entreaties. Then the negroes from Pipe Down began to send deputations over to beg my father to buy them. Philip Washington, a very tall, very black man, a splendid specimen of the negro race, after two generations of slavery, was their spokesman. My uncle had been devoted to Philip, and considered him far above the average negro in every way, and in his will had given him his freedom, along with two or three others; he pleaded the cause of his friends with much eloquence, saying they had fixed on him as the one owner they desired. Then my uncle, James L. Petigru, entered the lists, and appealed to my father's chivalry for his old and feeble sister-in-law, and to the intense feeling of the negroes, who had selected him for their future owner, and were perfectly miserable at his refusal — if it were a question of money, he argued, my father need not hesitate, as "Sister Ann" did not desire any cash payment; she greatly preferred a bond and mortgage, and the interest paid yearly, as that would be the best investment she could have. At last my father yielded, and made a small cash payment, giving his bond and a mortgage for the rest. The deed was done — the Pipe Down people were overjoyed, and the debt assumed. This debt it was which rendered my father's estate insolvent at the end of the war, for he died in 1864. The slaves having been freed, the property was gone, but the debt remained in mortgages on his landed estates, which had all to be sold. The plantations were: Chicora Wood, 890 acres, Ditchford, 350 acres, Exchange, 600 acres, Guendalos, 600 acres, Nightingale Hall, 400 acres, Waterford, 250 acres, beside Pipe Down itself. Also the two farms in Anson County, North Carolina, and our beautiful house in Charleston. Besides this, there were 6,000 acres of cypress timber at Britton's Neck; 5,000 acres of cypress and pine land near Carver's Bay; 300 acres at Canaan Seashore; house and 20 acres on Pawley's Island. Of all this principality, not one of the heirs got anything!

My mother's dower was all that could be claimed. In South Carolina the right of dower is one-third of the landed property, for life, or one-sixth, in fee simple. My mother preferred the last, and the Board of Appraisers found that the plantation Chicora Wood, where she had always lived, would represent a sixth value of the real estate, and that was awarded her as dower; but not an animal nor farm implement, no boats nor vehicles — just the land, with its dismantled dwelling-house. I tell this here, to explain how we came to face poverty at the end of the war.

CHAPTER II

PLANTER AND CITIZEN

NOW I must go back to my father's early life, for I left him just married, and bringing his beautiful bride from the gay life of the city to the intense quiet, as far as social joys went, of the country. It was wonderful that their marriage proved a success, and a great credit to them both. They were so absolutely different in tastes and ideals that each had to give up a great deal that they had dreamed of in matrimony; but their principles and standards being the same, things always came right in the end. My father was always a very public-spirited man, and interested in the good of his county and his State. Of course, all this public life necessitated constant and prolonged absences from home, and the rejoicing was great always, when the legislature adjourned and he returned from Columbia. He was a scientific rice-planter and agriculturist; he wrote articles for *De Bow's Review* that were regarded as authorities. His plantations were models of organization and management. All the negroes were taught a trade or to do some special work. On Chicora Wood there was a large carpenter's shop, where a great number of skilled men were always at work, under one head carpenter. Daddy Thomas was this head, during all my childhood, and he was a great person in my eyes. He was so dignified, and treated us young daughters of the house as though we were princesses; just the self-respecting manner of a noble courtier. His wife was the head nurse of the "sick-house," and the "children's house," also, so that she was also a personage — very black and tall, with a handkerchief turban of unusual height. We never went near her domain without returning with handsome presents of eggs, or potatoes, or figs, according to season, for Maum Phœbe was a very rich person and one of great authority. There were always four or five apprentices in the carpenter's shop, so year by year skilled men were turned out, not "jack-legs," which was Thomas Bonneau's epithet for the incompetent. Then the blacksmith-shop, under Guy Walker, was a most complete and up-to-date affair, and there young lads were always being taught to make horseshoes, and to shoe horses, and do all the necessary mending of wheels and axles and other ironwork used on a plantation.

The big flats and lighters needed to harvest the immense rice-crops were all made in the carpenter's shop, also the flood-gates necessary to let the water on and off the fields. These were called "trunks," and had to be made as tight as a fine piece of joiner's work. There was almost a fleet of rowboats, of all sizes, needed on the plantation for all purposes, also canoes, or dugouts, made from cypress logs. There was one dugout, *Rainbow*, capable of carrying several tierces of rice. When I was a child, the threshing of the rice from the straw was done in mills run by horse-power; before I can remember it was generally done by water-power. The men and women learned to work in the mill; to do the best ploughing; the best trenching with the hoe — perfectly straight furrows, at an even depth, so as to insure the right position for the sprouting grain; the most even and best sowing of the rice. Then, skilfully to take all the grass and weeds out with the sharp, tooth-shaped hoes, yet never touch or bruise the grain or its roots, the best cultivation of the crop. Also they learned to cut the rice most dexterously, with reap-hooks, and lay the long golden heads carefully on the stubble, so that the hot sun could get through and dry it, as would not be possible if it were laid on the wet earth, so that it could be tied in sheaves the next day. For all these operations prizes were offered every year — pretty bright-colored calico frocks to the women, and forks and spoons; and to the men fine knives, and other things that they liked — so that there was a great pride in being the prize ploughman, or prize sower, or harvest hand, for the year.

Only the African race, who seem by inheritance immune from the dread malarial fever, could have made it possible and profitable to clear the dense cypress swamps and cultivate them in rice by a system of flooding the fields from the river by canals, ditches, and flood-gates, draining off the water when necessary, and leaving these wonderfully rich lands dry for cultivation. It has been said that, like the pyramids, slave labor only could have accomplished it; be that as it may, at this moment one has the pain of watching the annihilation of all this work now, when the world needs food; now when the starving nations are holding out their hands to our country for food, thousands and thousands of acres of this fertile land are reverting to the condition of swamps: land capable of bringing easily sixty bushels of rice to the acre without fertilizer is growing up in reeds and rushes and marsh, the haunt of the alligator and the moccasin. The crane and the bittern are always there, the fish-hawk and the soaring eagle build their nests on the tall cypress-trees left here and there on the banks of the river; the beautiful wood-duck is also always there, and at certain seasons the big mallard or English duck come in great flocks; but, alas, they no longer come in clouds, as they used to do (so that a single shot has been known to kill sixty on the wing). For them too the country is ruined, for them too all is changed. Those that come do not stay. It was the abundant shattered rice of the culti- vated fields, flooded as soon as the harvest was over, which brought them in myriads from their nesting-grounds in the far north, to spend their winters in these fat feeding-grounds, in the con- genial climate of Carolina. Now there is no shattered rice on which to feed, and in their won- derful zigzag flight they stop a day or two to see if the abundance of which their forefathers have quacked to them has returned, and not find- ing it they pass on to Florida and other warm climes to seek their winter food. Thus this rich storehouse and granary is desolate. With the

modern machinery for making dikes and banks
these fields could be restored to a productive condition and made to produce again, without a very
heavy expenditure. But alas! those who owned
them had absolutely no money, and after the destruction of the banks and flood-gates by the
great storm of 1906 no restoration was made. A
few of the plantations in Georgetown County
have been bought by wealthy Northern men as
game-preserves. One multimillionaire, Emerson,
who bought a very fine rice-plantation, Prospect
Hill, formerly property of William Allston, has
some fields planted in rice every year, simply for
the ducks, the grain not being harvested at all,
but left to attract the flocks to settle down and
stay there, ready for the sportsman's gun.

Besides being a diligent, devoted, and scientific
planter and manager of his estates, my father was
greatly interested in the welfare of the poor whites
of the pineland, spoken of always scornfully by the
negroes as "Po' Buchra" — nothing could express
greater contempt. Negroes are by nature aristo-
crats, and have the keenest appreciation and perception of what constitutes a gentleman. The
poor whites of the low country were at a terrible
disadvantage, for they were never taught to do

anything; they only understood the simplest farm work, and there was no market for their labor, the land-owners having their own workers and never needing to hire these untrained hands, who in their turn looked down on the negroes, and held aloof from them. These people, the yeomanry of the country, were the descendants of the early settlers, and those who fought through the Revolution. They were, as a general rule, honest, law-abiding, with good moral standards. Most of them owned land, some only a few acres, others large tracts, where their cattle and hogs roamed unfed but fat. Some owned large herds, and even the poorest usually had a cow and pair of oxen, while all had chickens and hogs — but never a cent of money. They planted corn enough to feed themselves and their stock, sweet potatoes, and a few of the common vegetables. They never begged or made known their needs, except by coming to offer for sale very roughly made baskets of split white oak, or some coarsely spun yarn, for the women knew how to spin, and some of them even could weave. There was something about them that suggested a certain refinement, and one always felt they came from better stock, though they never seemed to trace back. Their respect

[18]

for the marriage vow, for instance, impressed one, and their speech was clear, good Anglo-Saxon, and their vocabulary included some old English words and expressions now obsolete. My father was most anxious to help them, and felt that to establish schools for them throughout the county would be the first step. In one of these schools a young girl proved such an apt scholar and learned so quickly all that she could acquire there that he engaged a place for her in a Northern school, and got the consent of her parents to her going, and she, being ambitious, was greatly pleased. He appointed a day to meet her in Georgetown, impressing on the parents to bring her in time for him to put her on the ship, before it sailed for New York. At the appointed time the parents arrived. My father asked for Hannah; the mother answered that they found they would miss Hannah too much, she was so smart and helpful, but they'd brought Maggie, and he could send *her* to school! My father was very angry; Hannah Mitchell was eighteen and clever and ambitious, while Maggie was fourteen, and dull and heavy-minded. Of course he did not send her. It was a great disappointment, for he had taken much trouble, and was willing to go to considerable expense to give Hannah the chance to develop, and hoped she would return prepared to teach in the school he had established. These people are still to be found in our pinelands, and have changed little.

The public roads were also my father's constant care, and all through that country were beautifully kept. The method was simple; each land-owner sent out twice a year a number of hands, proportioned to his land, and the different gentlemen took turns to superintend the work. Our top-soil goes down about two feet, before reaching clay. The roads were kept in fine condition by digging a good ditch on each side of a sixty-foot highway; the clay from the ditch being originally thrown into the middle of the road, and then twice a year those ditches were cleared out, and a little more clay from them thrown on the road each time. The great difficulty in road-making and road-keeping, as I know from my personal observation in the present, is not the amount of labor, but the proper, intelligent direction of the work. In my father's day, the office of road commissioner and supervisor were unpaid, and my father gave his time, work, and interest unstintedly.

My father's love of art, and of music, and of all

beauty was very great. It made all the difference in the world to us, his children, growing up in the country, so far from picture-galleries and concerts and every kind of music. At the sale of the Bonaparte collection of pictures in Baltimore my father commissioned the artist, Sully, to attend the sale and select and buy for him six pictures. Papa was much pleased with Mr. Sully's selection. They included:

"A Turk's Head," by Rembrandt.

"The Supper at Emmaus," by Gherardo del Notte.

"The Holy Family," a very beautiful Gobelin tapestry. For this picture Mr. Sully was offered double the price he paid before it left the gallery.

"Io," whom Juno in jealous rage had transformed into a white heifer. A very large and beautiful canvas, a landscape with the heifer ruminating in the foreground, watched by Cerberus, while on a mountainside Mercury sits playing on his flute, trying to lull him to sleep. (I still own this painting.)

"St. Paul on the Island of Melita," a very large canvas representing a group of shipwrecked mariners around a fire of sticks; in the midst stands the figure of St. Paul just shaking from his finger a viper, into the fire, very dramatic.

"St. Peter in Prison," awakened by the angel while his keepers sleep.

This is the match picture to the above and the same size.

These works of art on the walls of our country home awoke in us all an appreciation and recognition of fine paintings for which we can never be sufficiently grateful.

This great love for art and his confidence in its elevating influence is shown by his buying and having placed in the grounds of the State capitol a replica of Houdon's statue of Washington.

Another and most characteristic evidence is furnished by the following note from a friend, to whom I wrote, asking for some facts as to my father's public life, for I had thus far written of him entirely as I knew him in his family and home life, except for the bare outline by the dates of his election to different offices, and though I have no desire or intention of making this a history of his official and political career, feeling myself entirely unfitted for that, I felt I should give something to show his service in his own State. In reply Mr. Yates Snowden wrote:

"The day before your letter came my eye lit upon the invitation of R. F. W. Allston, president of the Carolina Art Association, inviting the members of the Convention Secession to visit the Gallery of Art in Meeting Street whilst deliberating here for the public weal. It is hoped that an hour bestowed occasionally in viewing some specimens of art, including Leutze's illustration of Jasper and the old Palmetto Fort, may contribute an agreeable diversion to the minds of gentlemen habitually engrossed in the discussion of grave concerns of state." — ("Journal of the (Secession) Convention," p. W225, April 1, 1861.)

I can quite imagine that this invitation was a source, to some of the members of that convention, of great amusement, as being most unsuitable to their frame of mind.

My father's full sympathy with the convention is shown by the following extract from Brant and Fuller's "Eminent and Representative Men of the Carolinas":

"Robert Francis Withers Allston, South Carolina statesman, scholar, and agriculturist, was born April 21, 1801. . . . During the nullifica-

[23]

tion era and for many years afterward Mr. Allston was deputy adjutant-general of the militia,
and from 1841 to 1864 was one of the trustees of
South Carolina College at Columbia. . . . In
politics he belonged to the Jefferson and Calhoun
school, believing in the complete sovereignty of
the States."

During his prolonged absences in Columbia my
father did not like to leave my mother alone on
the plantation, with no one but the negroes to
care for the children, so he secured a good, reliable
Irishwoman to take charge of the children and
the nursery, with the others under her. Strange
to say, this was never resented, and Mary O'Shea
stayed with us about fifteen years, when some of
her kinfolk called her away. We called her
"May" and were devoted to her. She had her
trials, for my father did not approve of fire in the
room where the children slept, and this, along
with the open window, was a terrible ordeal to
May. The day-nursery, with its roaring open
wood-fire, only made the contrast more distressing
to her; she never became reconciled to it, and I
only wonder that she stayed all those years. As
soon as the older children were big enough, we

had an English governess—Miss Wells first, and afterward Miss Ayme.

I have asked my brother, Charles Petigru Allston, to write for me what he remembered of my father, and I will insert here what he has written for me.

CHAPTER III

MY BROTHER'S NARRATIVE

M Y holiday, the months of December, 1863, and January, 1864, were passed with my father on the coast, where he had planting, salt boiling, and freighting up the rivers, to look after. Salt was a very scarce article at that time, and my father had it boiled from sea-water on the salt creeks of the Waccamaw seashore, behind Pawley's Island. The vats were made chiefly of old mill boilers, cut in half and mounted on brick, with furnace below for wood, and a light shed above, to protect from the weather. A scaffold was built out in the salt creek, and a pump placed there to lift the water about twenty feet, and from the pump a wooden trough carried the water to the boilers, some 300 yards away, in the forest. At flood-tide, when the water came in from the sea, was the best time to pump, as the water had then more salt and less of the seepage water from the marshlands. Sometimes, when a man was upon the scaffold, pumping, a federal gunboat, lying off the coast, would throw a shell over the island, which cut off the sight of the works, in the direction of the smoke from the boiling vats; when this happened the man came down in wild haste and made for the brush. These interruptions became so frequent that finally the boiling had to be done at night, when the smoke was not visible. My father sent me over to inspect the salt-works and report to him more than once, so that I was familiar with the situation. Wagons came long distances from the interior to buy or barter for salt. This work was carried on entirely by negroes, without any white man in charge. My father had the faculty for organization, and his negro men were remarkably well trained, intelligent, and self-reliant. Another work which he instituted and developed was the transporting of rice and salt up the rivers to the railroad. The ports, being blockaded, and no railroad within forty miles, it became necessary to make some outlet for the rice-crop to get to market and to the army. He had two lighters built, which were decked over and secured from weather, and carried from 150 to 200 tierces (600 pounds each) of clean or marketable rice. On each lighter he put a captain, with a crew of eight men. These lighters were loaded at the rice-mill and taken up the Pee Dee River, to the railroad bridge near Mars Bluff, to Society Hill, and sometimes to Cheraw. It was a long, hard trip, and when the freshet was up it seemed sometimes to be impossible to carry a loaded barge against the current, by hand — but it was done. At such times the only progress was made by carrying a line ahead, making fast to a tree on the river-bank, and then all hands warping the boat up by the capstan; then make fast and carry the line ahead again. The crew were all able men. They had plenty to eat and seemed to enjoy themselves. I have often been with my father when the boats returned from a trip and the captain came to make his report; it was worth listening to; the most minute account of the trip, with all its dangers and difficulties. There was seldom a charge of any serious character against any of the crew; each knew that such a charge made by the captain meant the immediate discharge from the crew and a return to field work.

My father also sent rice up the Black River to the Northeastern Railroad at Kingstree, and finally built a warehouse, making a new station, which is now Salter's; here he put a very intelligent negro, Sam Maham, in charge; he received the rice from the captains of the river-craft, and delivered it to the railroad on orders, and I have never heard a word of complaint against him. Black River, however, had to be navigated by smaller craft than the Pee Dee, open flats, boats square at each end, and 50 feet long by 12 feet wide. I well remember the report made by the captain of the first crew sent up Black River. It was thrilling in parts. He had to cut his way through after leaving the lower river, which was open for navigation. The river had never been used high up for that sort of craft, and was full of logs, etc.; besides, in places it was difficult to find the right channel, and his description of going through a section where the river was broken up by low islands, or shoals into several apparent channels, all of which were shallow, except one, was most exciting. None of these men had ever been on this river or in that locality before, and only the drilling and direction given them by my father could have carried them through; but they went through, and after that there was a regular line going. But these flats being smaller and open and no decks, were much more liable to damage the cargo; still very little was lost, strange to say. They had good sail-cloth covers, and the crews took an interest in the work. The captain and crew making the best record were always well rewarded.

I became familiar with all this work during the winter of 1863–64. My father wanted me to learn as much as possible of each branch of the work, and knew how to direct my attention to the chief details to be studied and worked out.

At night we sat together and had milk and potatoes, with sassafras tea for supper, and it was very good. One who has never had to depend on sassafras tea does not know how good it is. My father had many opportunities for getting in all the supplies that he wanted, as well as for making a good deal of money by exchanging his rice and salt for cotton, and then sending the cotton out by the blockade-runners to Nassau; but he was opposed to the running of the blockade for private gain. How often as we sat by the fire in the evenings did he talk to me on that and other subjects of public interest. His idea was that the Confederate Government should control the cotton; buy it up at home, pay for it in gold, ship it out by blockade-runners, sell it in Europe for the government, and bring in such supplies as were most needed — medicines, shoes, clothes, as well as arms, etc. In this way, he said, the government would be free from the horde of speculators who were making fortunes out of our misfortunes, and thus be able to build up a financial standing in Europe that would go far toward deciding the status of the Confederate States. He was most earnest on this subject, and I know that he made more than one trip to Richmond for the purpose of urging some such measure on President Davis, but he returned disappointed, and I remember after one trip he seemed entirely hopeless as to the outcome. Feeling, as he did, he would never avail himself of the many opportunities which offered, except to get such things as were prime necessities. In February, 1864, I returned to my school in Abbeville district. I drove away from the Chicora house on my way to the railroad, forty miles distant, leaving my father standing on the platform at the front door. That was my last sight of him. He died in April, 1864, and though I was written for, the mails and transportation were so slow that he was buried before I got home.

I returned to school after being at home a few weeks in April, and remained until the following October, when the school was dismissed. The call for recruits for the army was now from sixteen years up, and would include many who were at the school. I went to my mother at Society Hill and was to get ready to join the corps of State Cadets.

While I was at Society Hill my mother heard from the overseer at Chicora Wood, that he had some trouble about repairing the freight-lighters. This being a most important matter and requiring to be promptly attended to, my mother decided to send me down to see if I could help the overseer. So I started off on a little brown horse to ride the ninety miles down to the rice country. I arrived safely, and after a few days began to make headway with the work. The largest lighter had been in the water a good long time and was very heavy to haul out, but was badly in need of repairing. It was my first experience of unwilling labor; the hands were sulky. My father's talks and teaching now came in to the aid of my own knowledge of the negro nature, and before long I had the big lighter hauled up, high and dry. We had and could get no oakum for calking, but my father had devised a very respectable substitute in cypress bark; it was stripped from the tree and then broken, somewhat as flax is, and then worked in the hands until quite pliable; this did wonderfully well, though it did not last as well as oakum. If pitch was freely applied to the freshly calked seams a very good job was made. We got the lighter calked and cleaned and simply painted, and put back in the water ready for work.

I then returned to my mother at Society Hill and remained there until I joined the Arsenal Cadets, and we entered the active service.

My father's eldest brother, Joseph, while a student at the South Carolina College was appointed lieutenant in the United States army by President Madison and served in Florida in the War of 1812. He attained the rank of general, and all his life was given that title. Though he died at forty-five he had been married three times, his last wife, Mary Allan, only, having children. She had two sons, Joseph Blyth and William Allan. She lived only a few years after her husband, and the little boys were left to the guardianship of my father and the care of my mother, and Chicora Wood was their home until they grew up. Joseph Blyth Allston was a gifted man, a clever lawyer and eloquent pleader. His literary talent was above the ordinary; he has written some poems of great beauty; "Stack Arms" and the longer poem, "Sumter," deserve a high place in the war poetry of the South. By the merest chance a sketch of my father, written by him, at the request of some one whose individuality is unknown to me, has fallen into my hands at this moment, and I gladly quote from it here, leaving out only the repetitions of facts already stated:

"All the offices held by Robert F. W. Allston in the State were filled by him with credit to himself and usefulness to the country, but his private virtues gave him a much more enduring claim to the regard of his contemporaries and of posterity. In the forties he had been offered the office of governor and had peremptorily declined it. This was not for want of ambition, but because he had dined at Colonel Hampton's a few days before, in company with Mr. Hammond, who aspired to that office, and without formally pledging himself, had tacitly acquiesced in his candidacy. A liberal economy marked his expenditures, and a cultivated hospitality made his home the centre of a large circle of friends. The rector of the parish (Prince Frederick's) dined with him every Sunday, with his wife. At dessert the Methodist minister generally arrived from some other appointment, took a glass of wine, and then preached to the negroes in the plantation chapel in the avenue, constructed in the Gothic style by his negro carpenters, under his direction.

"He did much to improve the breeds of cattle, sheep, and swine in his neighborhood, and was a constant correspondent of the Bureau of Agriculture at Washington. He was an active member of the South Carolina Jockey Club, of the St. Cecilia Society, and of the South Carolina Historical Society of Charleston; of the Winyah Indigo Society of Georgetown, of which he was long president; of the Hot and Hot Fish Club of Waccamaw; the Winyah and All Saints Agricultural Society, and the Agricultural Association of the Southern States. He was also a member of the Order of Masons.

"He was an eminently successful rice-planter and made many improvements in the cultivation of that crop and the drainage of the rice-lands.

"'Allston on Sea-Coast Crops' is the title of a valuable treatise on this subject, which unfortunately is now out of print. Yet one of his best overseers, when asked if he was not a great planter, replied:

"'No, sir, he is no planter at all.'

" 'To what, then, do you attribute his great success?'

" 'To his power of organization, sir, and the system and order which he enforces on all whom he controls.'

"That was indeed the keynote of his character. He was most regular in his own habits, and all within his reach felt the influence of his example. Especially marked was it upon the negroes whom he owned. Even at this day (1900) they show by their thrift and industry the influence of his training and speak of him with pride and affection.

"Political matters and his duty as a member of the Protestant Episcopal Church often called him to the North, and sometimes he took a trip there with his family for pleasure. In 1855 he took his wife and eldest daughter abroad, and they travelled all over the Continent. He took a prize at the Paris Exposition that year for rice grown on his plantation, Chicora Wood, Pee Dee—a silver medal. The rice was presented to the war office, Department of Algeria, in the autumn, and was in such perfect preservation (in glass jars) that in the succeeding year it was again exhibited under the auspices of the Department of War, and was adjudged worthy of a gold medal [which has been placed in the National Museum in Washington for the present. — E. W. A. P.].

"Usually, however, he spent the summers on the sea-beach of Pawley's Island, and enforced by example as well as precept the duty of the landowner to those dependent on him. Here he fished and hunted deer, of which he has been known to send home two by 10 A.M., shot on his way to the plantation. Here he was within easy reach of his estates, and could exercise an intelligent and elevating control over the 600 negroes who called him master. This beautiful and bountiful country, watered by the noble stream of the Waccamaw and the Pee Dee, and washed by the waves of the Atlantic Ocean, was very near to his heart. And here, amid the scenes in which he had spent his life, he died at his home, Chicora Wood, April 7, 1864, and lies buried in the yard of the old Church of Prince George, Winyah, at Georgetown, South Carolina." — (*Extract from paper by Jos. Blyth Allston.*)

And now I must leave this imperfect portrait of my father. Of his illness and death I shall tell elsewhere.

His taking away was softened to me afterward

by the feeling that he did not live to see the downfall of the hopes he had cherished for the success of the Confederacy, nor the humiliation of the State he had so loved, when its legislative halls were given up to the riotous caricature of State government by the carpetbaggers and negroes, who disported themselves as officials of the State of South Carolina, from the surrender of Lee until 1876, when Wade Hampton redeemed the State from its degradation.

It was only Hampton's wonderful power and influence over the men, brave as lions, whom he had led in battle, that prevented awful bloodshed and woe. In 1876 I heard a high-spirited, passionate man, who had been one of Butler's most daring scouts, say, when hearing of a youth whose front teeth had been knocked out by a negro on the street: "Why, I would let a negro knock me down and trample on me, without lifting a hand, for Hampton has said: 'Forbear from retaliation, lift not a hand, no matter what the provocation; the State must be redeemed!'" And, thank God, it was redeemed! Those brave men did not suffer and bear insult and assault in vain. My faith in my father is so great that I cannot help feeling that if he had lived he would have been able to prevent things from reaching the depths they did. Of one thing I am certain, that if his life had been spared until after the war we as a family would not have been financially ruined. He would have been able to evolve some system by which, with his own people, he could have worked the free labor successfully and continued to make large crops of rice and corn, as he had done all through the war. His was a noble life, and Milton's words come to my mind:

"There's no place here for tears or beating of the breast."

PART II

MY MOTHER

CHAPTER IV

EARLY DAYS AND OLD FIELD SCHOOL

MY mother, Adèle Petigru, was the granddaughter of Jean Louis Gibert, one of the Pasteurs du Desert, who brought the last colony of Huguenots to South Carolina in April, 1764, after enduring persecution in France, holding his little flock together through great peril and having the forbidden services of his church in forests, in barns, at the midnight hour, in order to escape imprisonment and death. There was a price set upon his head for some years before he made up his mind to leave his beloved land and escape with his little band of faithful to America. These perils and the martyrdom of some of his followers is told in "Les Frères Gibert." It is a thrilling story, but too long to tell here. The two brothers, Etienne and Jean Louis, escaped to England, the little flock following one by one. King George III made a grant of land in South Carolina to Jean Louis for the settlement of the colony. He retained Etienne in England as his chaplain.

The difficulties and setbacks encountered by the little band were most harrowing and discouraging, but at last they reached the shores of what was to them the promised land, and disembarked at Charleston, South Carolina, April 14, 1764, from which city they made their way some 300 miles into the interior of the State where their grant was. Their difficulties were by no means over; indeed, to them it seemed sometimes as if they were only begun. The wild rugged wilderness where they were to establish themselves, they called by the names they had left in their beautiful France, New Bordeaux and Abbeville, and they set to work to clear land and plant the cuttings of grape-vines to make wine, and the cuttings of mulberry to carry on the manufacture of silk, which were their industries at home. It is hard for us now to realize what they had to encounter and endure — wild beasts, Indians, difficulties of transportation, of transforming the big trees of the forest into lumber suitable to building houses; but all these they conquered. They built homes, they planted vineyards and orchards and mulberry-groves, and succeeded in the manufacture of silk with their spinning-wheels and hand-looms. There is at the old home place in Abbeville now one of the little spinning-wheels with which the silk was spun, that the colony sent with pride as a gift to be made into a dress for the royal wardrobe of the Queen of England.

My great-grandfather was a man of executive ability and strength, with that personal charm which made him intensely beloved and revered by his little flock; and they prospered as long as he lived, but, alas, his life was cut short by an unfortunate accident. He had brought with him from France a devoted and capable attendant, Pierre Le Roy, who in this wilderness filled many and diverse offices; he delighted to vary the often very limited diet of the pasteur by preparing for him dainty dishes of mushrooms with which he was familiar in the old country. There are many varieties here unknown there, and any one who knows this delicious but dangerous vegetable, knows how easily confounded are the good and the poisonous; the deadly Aminita resembles very closely one of the best edible mushrooms; we know not exactly how, but one night the dainty dish proved fatal to the great and good pasteur, and his flock was left desolate in August, 1773, just nine years after their arrival in the New World.

Jean Louis Gibert had married Isabeau Boutiton, a fellow emigrant and sister of his assistant minister, Pierre Boutiton. She was left a widow very young, with two little daughters, Louise and Jeanne, and one son, Joseph, to struggle with the difficult new life. I cannot pursue the fortunes of the colony, but without the leader and counsellor on whom they leaned the colony soon began to disintegrate and disperse, and their descendants are now scattered all over the country. But of this I am sure, wherever they have gone they have carried their strong, upright influence, always raising the standards and ideals of the communities they entered.

Little Louise Gibert very early married William Pettigrew, a blue-eyed, fair-haired young neighbor, who was charmed by her dark beauty. His grandparents had come from Ireland and settled in Pennsylvania, from which State their sons had scattered, Charles settling in North Carolina, where he was to become the first bishop of the Episcopal Church, and William settling in South Carolina as a farmer.

They had a large family, four sons and five daughters:

James Louis, who became a very distinguished
man, a lawyer.

John, clever and witty, but the ne'er-do-well
of the family.

Tom, who died a captain in the U. S. navy.

Charles, who graduated at West Point.

The daughters were:

Jane Gibert, who married John North.

Mary, who never married.

Louise, married Philip Johnston Porcher.

Adèle, married Robert Francis Withers Allston.

Harriet, married Henry Deas Lesesne.

The sisters were all women of rare beauty, but
Mary. Outsiders never could decide which was
the most beautiful, but, of course, each family
thought their own mother entitled to the golden
apple. My mother was painted by the artist
Sully when she was twenty-two, just a year after
the birth of her first child, Benjamin, when she
was so ill that her hair was cut, so she appears in
the portrait with short brown curls, and is very
lovely. There is a portrait of her painted by
Flagg, in middle life. When she died in her
eighty-seventh year she was still beautiful, with
brown, wavy hair only sprinkled with gray.

The tradition in my mother's father's family
was that the Pettigrews had come from France

after the Revocation of the Edict of Nantes, and had gone to Scotland, when they had changed the spelling of the name from Petigru, and had eventually moved to Ireland. This idea was, of course, pleasant to the little Frenchwoman, and when her eldest son, James Louis, grew up and proposed to change the spelling of his name and revert to the French spelling she was delighted, and the father consented that the children should spell the name as they preferred, but he declined to change his. So on his and his wife's tombstone in the most interesting little God's acre at the old home in Abbeville, his name is William Pettigrew, while all his children are recorded as Petigru. My mother said to me not long before her death that she felt it had been a mistake, as there was no survivor of the Petigru name, all the sons having died. But I do not agree with her, for my uncle, James L. Petigru, was a great man — heart, soul, and mind — and left a mark in his State, having codified her laws with knowledge and wisdom. He was almost the only man in Charleston who was opposed to secession, — I may almost say the only man in the State.* But he was so revered

---

* I remember now two other men who were opposed to the war — Nicholas Williams of Society Hill, and Gov. Perry of Greenville.

and beloved that, at a time when party feeling
was intense, he walked out of his pew in St.
Michael's Church (which he never failed to occupy
on Sunday) the first time the Prayer for the President of the United States was left out of the service, and no one ever said one word of criticism or
disapproval. In a period when party politics ran
high and bitter feeling was intense, it was a wonderful tribute to a man's character and integrity
that, even though running counter to the intense
united feeling of the community, love and respect
for him should have protected him from attack.

My mother always talked with great pleasure
of her early life. She spoke with admiration and
love which amounted to adoration of her "little
mother." Her father took second place always in
her narrative, though he was a most delightful
companion — very clever and full of wit, a great
reader, and it was his habit to read aloud in the
evenings, while the family sat around the fire,
each one with some appointed task. The elder
girls sewed, while all the children had their baskets
of cotton to pick, for in those days the gin had
not been invented and the seed had to be carefully
picked from the cotton by hand! It would seem
a weary task to us, but they regarded it as a

game, and ran races as to who should pick the most during the long winter evenings while my grandfather read Milton, Wordsworth, Shakespeare, and other masters of literature. When one contrasts those evenings, those influences on the minds of children, with the amusements and diversions deemed necessary to the young of the present day, one does not wonder at the pleasure-loving race we are becoming. Add to this that there were no little story-books to dissipate the minds of children. My mother's ideal of a story-book was her beloved Plutarch's "Lives," and I remember still with intense regret her disappointment when, I having accomplished the task of learning to read fluently, she one morning placed in my lap a large volume with very good print, and turned to the Life of Themistocles, which she had so loved. Perhaps if it had not been for the long s's which adorned this beautiful edition of Plutarch it might have been more of a success, but at the end of the half-hour I announced that I saw no pleasure in such a dull book. . . . I would gladly read to her from one of my story-books, and then she would see what a really nice book was. My dear mother was so pained. She had had the same experience with the older children, but she thought me very bright and felt sure that she would find a congenial mind in her "little Bessie." Seeing how hurt she was and that she had set her heart on that special book, I did not insist on my book but came every day and read the Plutarch aloud; but I never enjoyed it, which she could never understand.

This thing of bringing all reading matter presented to a child down to its level is a great mistake; it lowers ideals and taste. Stories while you are a child, and then romances, novels, detective tales, corrupt the taste until it is so reduced that there are not many young people now who can read Scott's novels with any more pleasure than I read Plutarch at ten. My mother's school was the old field school of the long ago. The country was thinly settled and the schools widely separated, so that children had to make an all-day business of it. The nearest school to the family home was on Long Cane, three miles away, and mamma, at first accompanied by an older sister and brother, later alone, walked three miles to school every day. She took her little basket of lunch, a substantial one, for she did not get home again until late afternoon. It is quite surprising to find what excellent instruction was given in these "old field schools." Education was not so widely diversified, but it was more thorough and of a higher kind, as far as it went.

Mamma learned to prove sums by "casting out the nines" in a wonderful way, which no one else that I ever saw knew anything about. Her mind was stored with treasures of good poetry which she had been required to memorize in school. On her solitary walk home she was never lonely. The birds and the little inhabitants of the woods were her delight. At a big chestnut-tree about a mile from home she had special friends — two squirrels who ran down from their castle in the top of the tree when they heard her coming, and she always reserved some of her lunch for them. She sat at the root of the tree and played with them until she saw the sun about to sink below the horizon, when she picked up her little school-bag and started at a run for the last stretch of her way home.

CHAPTER V

DADDY TOM AND DADDY PRINCE — DEATH OF LITTLE MOTHER SO BELOVED

THE farms of the up-country as a rule required few hands, and so each farmer owned only a few negroes, and, of course, the relations between master and slave were different from those in the low-country, where each plantation had a hundred or more negroes, which necessitated separate villages, where the negroes lived more or less to themselves. In the up-country it was more like one large family. In my mother's home there were three quite remarkable, tall, fine-looking, and very intelligent Africans who had been bought by her grandfather from the ship which brought them to this country. Tom, Prince, and Maria — they occupied an important place in my mother's recollections of her early childhood. They had been of a royal family in their own land, and had been taken in battle by an enemy tribe with which they were at war, and sold to a slave-ship. No one ever doubted their claim to royal blood, for they were so superior to the ordinary Africans brought out. They were

[53]

skilled in the arts of their own country, and had artistic tastes and clever hands. Daddy Tom and Daddy Prince told tales of their wild forests, which the children were never tired of hearing nor they of telling. Maum Maria made wonderful baskets and wove beautiful rugs from the rushes that grew along Long Cane Creek. One day as she sat on the ground weaving a rug which she had hung from a tree, and my mother was listening to her stories of her home in Africa, the little girl said in a voice of sympathy: "Maum 'Ria, you must be dreadfully sorry they took you away from all that, and brought you to a strange land to work for other people." Maum Maria stopped her work, rose to her full height — she was very tall and straight — clasped her hands and said, dropping a deep courtesy as she spoke: "My chile, ebery night on my knees I tank my Hebenly Father that he brought me here, for without that I wud neber hev known my Saviour !" She remained, hands clasped, and a look of ecstasy on her face, for some time before she sat down and resumed her work, and the little girl, greatly impressed, asked no more questions that day. When grandmother died, she left these three free, with a little sum to be given them yearly; not much, for she had little to leave. Daddy Tom took his freedom, but Daddy Prince and Maum Maria said they were grateful to their beloved mistress, but they would rather remain just as they were; they had all they needed and were happy and loved their white family, and they did not want to make any change.

My grandfather Pettigrew, with all his charming qualities of wit and good humor, had no power to make or keep money. And among the few sad memories my mother had of her childhood was that of seeing her beloved little mother sitting at the window looking out, while tears coursed down her cheeks, as she saw the sheriff taking off all their cattle, and two families of their negroes to be sold! . . . her husband having gone security for a worthless neighbor. My mother told it with tears, even when she was very old, the scene seemed to come so vividly before her of her mother's silent grief.

It is curious to me that my paternal grandfather, Ben Allston, also lost his plantation for a security debt, having signed a paper when he was under age for a cousin who was in trouble pecuniarily. Grandfather was advised by a lawyer to contest the matter, as he had been a minor and it was not valid, but he would not avail himself of that plea, I am thankful to say, and lost the beautiful and valuable plantation which he had inherited, Brook Green on the Waccamaw. That is the only point of similarity between my two grandfathers, however, as they were totally different types, one Scotch-Irish, the other pure English.

The little Frenchwoman, so beloved by her children, did not live to show any sign of age, and the memory remained with my mother of her beauty, her olive skin and black hair, in which no strands of white appeared, and her graceful, small, active figure and tiny hands and feet. She always spoke broken English, but, as her husband did not speak or understand French, she never spoke it with her children through courtesy to him, and none of them spoke French. Her illness was short and the family had no idea it was to be fatal, but evidently she recognized it, for she called my mother and kissed her, and said: "My child, I want to tell you that you have been my greatest comfort. I want you to remember that always."

CHAPTER VI

MARRIAGE

AFTER the mother's death the home seemed very desolate; and when the eldest brother's, James L. Petigru's, wife proposed most generously to take the younger girls to live with them in Charleston, so that their education might be carried on, their father gladly consented, and my mother from that time lived with her brother in Charleston until her marriage, having the best teachers that the city afforded and enjoying the most charming and witty social surroundings. Aunt Petigru, though a beauty and belle, was a great invalid, so that the care of the house and her two young children came much on the sisters-in-law. Louise, two years older than my mother, married first and was established in her own home. After two years in society, which was very gay then, my mother became engaged to Robert Allston. When the family heard of the engagement they were greatly disturbed that my mother should contemplate burying her beauty and brilliant social gifts in the country, and her sister Louise thought fit to remonstrate, being a matron properly established in her city residence. She made a formal visit and opened her batteries at once.

"My dear Adèle, I have come to remonstrate with you on this extraordinary announcement you have made! You cannot think of accepting this young man. Mr. Allston lives winter and summer in the country. He will take you away from all your friends and family. That he is good-looking I grant you, and I am told he is a man of means; but it is simply madness for you with your beauty and your gifts to bury yourself on a rice-plantation. Perhaps I would not feel so shocked and surprised if you did not have at your feet one of the very best matches in the city. As it is, I feel I should be criminal if I let you make this fatal mistake without doing all I can to prevent it. If you accept Mr. Blank, you will have one of the most beautiful homes in the city. You will have ample means at your command and you will be the centre of a brilliant social circle. My dear sister, my love for you is too great for me to be silent. I must warn you. I must ask you why you are going to do this dreadful thing?"

My mother was at first much amused; but as

my aunt continued to grow more and more excited, contrasting her fate as my father's wife with the rosy picture of what it would be if she accepted the city lover, mamma said: "Louise, you want to know why I am going to marry Robert Allston? I will tell you: — because he is as obstinate as the devil. In our family we lack will-power; that is our weakness."

My aunt rose with great dignity, saying: "I will say good morning. Your reason is as extraordinary as your action." And she swept out of the room, leaving my mother master of the field.

It was indeed a brave thing for my mother to do, to face the lonely, obscure life, as far as society went, of a rice-planter's wife. She had been born in the country and lived there until she was fifteen, but it was a very different country from that to which she was going. It was in the upper part of the State, the hill country, where there were farms instead of plantations, and there were pleasant neighbors, the descendants of the French colony, all around, and each farmer had only one or two negroes, as the farms were small. In the rice country the plantations were very large, hundreds of acres in each, requiring hundreds of negroes to work them. And, the plantations being so big, the neighbors were far away and few in number. Whether my mother had any realization of the great difference I do not know. I hope she never repented her decision. I know she was very much in love with her blue-eyed, blond, silent suitor. They were complete contrasts and opposites in every way. Papa outside was considered a severe, stern man, but he had the tenderness of a very tender woman if you were hurt or in trouble — only expression was difficult to him, whereas to my mother it was absolutely necessary to express with a flow of beautiful speech all she felt.

They were married at St. Michael's Church, Charleston, April 21, 1832, and went into the country at once. There was a terrible storm of wind and rain that day, which seemed to the disapproving family an appropriate sign of woe. But it was only the feminine members of the family who were so opposed to my father. My uncle approved of mamma's choice, for he recognized in my father rare qualities of mind and spirit and that thing we call character which is so hard to define.

My uncle feared my mother would find only raw, untrained servants in her new home, so he gave her a well-trained maid and seamstress to whom she was accustomed, and who was devoted to her. Maum Lavinia was a thoroughly trained, competent house-servant, and must have been a great comfort, though she had a terrible temper. She married on the plantation and had a large family, dying only a few years ago, keeping all her faculties to extreme age. One of her grandsons is a prosperous, respected man in New York now, Hugh Roberton. I keep track of all the descendants of our family servants, and it gives me great pleasure when they make good and do credit to their ancestry. It does not always happen. In so many instances, to my great regret, they have fallen in character and good qualities instead of rising; — without training or discipline that is to be expected.

Mamma has told me of her dismay when she found what a big household she had to manage and control. Not long after they were married she went to my father, almost crying, and remonstrated: "There are too many servants; I do not know what to do with them. There is Mary, the cook; Milly, the laundress; Caroline, the housemaid; Cinda, the seamstress; Peter, the butler; Andrew, the second dining-room man; Aleck, the coachman; and Moses, the gardener. And George, the scullion, and the boy in the yard besides! I cannot find work for them! After breakfast, when they line up and ask, 'Miss, wha' yu' want me fu' do to-day?' I feel like running away. Please send some of them away, for Lavinia is capable of doing the work of two of them. Please send them away, half of them, at least."

But papa made her understand that he could not. These were house-servants; they had been trained for the work, even if they were not efficient and well trained. It would be a cruelty to send them into the field, to work which they were not accustomed to. Then he said: "As soon as you get accustomed to the life here you will know there is plenty for them to do. The house is large and to keep it perfectly clean takes constant work. Then there is the constant need of having clothes cut and made for the babies and little children on the place; the nourishment, soup, etc., to be made and sent to the sick. You will find that there is really more work than there are hands for, in a little while." And truly she found it so. But it took all her own precious time to direct and plan and carry out the work. The calls to do something which seemed important and necessary were incessant. One day my father came in and asked her to go with him to see a very ill man. She answered: "My dear Mr. Urston" (she always called papa Mr. Allston, but she said it so fast that it sounded like that), "I know nothing about sickness, and there is no earthly use for me to go with you. I have been having the soup made and sending it to him regularly, but I cannot go to see him, for I can do him no good." He answered with a grave, hurt look: "You are mistaken; you can do him good. At any rate, it is my wish that you go." Mamma got her hat and came down the steps full of rebellion, but silent. He helped her into the buggy and they drove off down the beautiful avenue of live oaks, draped with gray moss, out to the negro quarter, which is always called by them "the street."

The houses were built regularly about fifty yards apart on each side of a wide road, with fruit-trees on each side. There are generally about twelve houses on each side, so that it makes a little village. On Chicora Wood plantation there were three of these settlements, a little distance apart, each on a little elevation with good Southern exposure, and all named. One was called California, one Aunty Phibby Hill, and one Crick

Hill, because Chapel Creek, a beautiful stream of water, ran along parallel with it and very near. In California, which was the middle settlement, was the hospital, called by the darkies "the sickhouse." To this, which was much larger than the other houses, built for one family each, my father drove. He helped mamma out and they entered; the room was large and airy, and there on one of the beds lay an ill man with closed eyes and labored breathing; one could not but see that death was near. He appeared unconscious, with a look of great pain on his face. My father called his name gently, "Pompey." He opened his eyes and a look of delight replaced the one of pain. "My marster!" he exclaimed. "Yu cum! O, I tu glad! I tink I bin gwine, widout see yu once more."

Papa said: "I've brought something good for you to look upon, Pompey. I brought your young mistress to see you," and he took mamma's hand and drew her to the side of the bed where Pompey could see her without effort.

His whole face lit up with pleasure as he looked and he lifted up his hands and exclaimed: "My mistis! I tank de Lawd. He let me lib fu' see you! 'Tis like de light to my eye. God bless you, my missis." And turning his eyes to papa, he said: "Maussa, yu sure is chuse a beauty! 'Tis like de face of a angel! I kin res' better now, but, my marster, I'm goin'! I want yu to pray fur me."

So papa knelt by the bed and offered a fervent prayer that Pompey, who had been faithful in all his earthly tasks, should receive the great reward, and that he might be spared great suffering and distress in his going. Then he rose and pressed the hand which was held out to him, and went out followed by my mother. As they drove home she was filled with penitence and love. She wanted to express both, but as she glanced at my father she saw that his mind was far away and she could not. He was, in mind, with the dying man; he was full of self-questioning and solemn thought: "Had he been as faithful to every duty through life as Pompey in his humbler sphere had been?" No thought of his bride came to him.

At last she spoke and said: "I thank you for having made me come with you, and I beg you to forgive my petulance about coming. I did not understand." He pressed her hand and kissed her but spoke no word, and they returned to the house in silence.

[65]

My heart has always been filled with sympathy for my mother when she told me these things of her early life, for I was very like her, and I do not know how she stood that stern silence which came over papa when he was moved. And yet I adored him and I think she did, but all the same it must have been hard.

She found the life on the plantation a very full one and intensely interesting, but not at all the kind of life she had ever dreamed of or expected, a life full of service and responsibility. But where was the reading and study and self-improvement which she had planned? Something unexpected was always turning up to interrupt the programme laid out by her; little did she suspect that her mind and soul were growing apace in this apparently inferior life, as they could never have grown if her plans of self-improvement and study had been carried out.

CHAPTER VII

MOVE TO CANAAN — AUNT BLYTHE

THE cultivation of rice necessitated keeping the fields flooded with river water until it became stagnant, and the whole atmosphere was polluted by the dreadful smell. No white person could remain on the plantation without danger of the most virulent fever, always spoken of as "country fever." So the planters removed their families from their beautiful homes the last week in May, and they never returned until the first week in November, by which time cold weather had come and the danger of malarial fever gone. The formula was to wait for a black frost before moving; I believe that is purely a local expression; three white frosts make a black frost; that means that all the potato vines and all the other delicate plants had been killed so completely that the leaves were black.

At the end of May my father's entire household migrated to the sea, which was only four miles to the east of Chicora as the crow flies, but was only to be reached by going seven miles in a row-boat and four miles by land. The vehicles, horses, cows, furniture, bedding, trunks, provisions were all put into great flats, some sixty by twenty feet, others even larger, at first dawn, and sent ahead. Then the family got into the rowboat and were rowed down the Pee Dee, then through Squirrel Creek, with vines tangled above them and water-lilies and flags and wild roses and scarlet lobelia all along the banks, and every now and then the hands would stop their song a moment to call out: "Missy, a alligator!" And there on the reeds and marsh in some sunny cove lay a great alligator basking in the sun, fast asleep. As soon as the sound of the oars reached him, he would plunge into the water, making great waves on which the boat rose and fell in a way suggestive of the ocean itself. The way was teeming with life; birds of every hue and note flew from tree to tree on the banks; here and there on top of a tall cypress a mother hawk could be seen sitting on her nest, looking down with anxious eye, while around, in ever-narrowing circles, flew her fierce mate, with shrill cries, threatening death to the intruder. No one who has not rowed through these creeks in the late spring or early summer can imagine the abundance and variety of life everywhere. On every log floating down the stream or lodged along the shore, on such a summer day rows of little turtles can be seen fast asleep, just as many as the log will hold, ranging from the size of a dinner-plate to a dessert-plate, only longer than they are broad — the darkies call them "cooters" (they make a most delicious soup or stew) — so many it is hard to count the number one sees in one trip. Besides all this, there is the less-pleasing sight of snakes on the banks and sometimes on the tree overhanging the water, also basking in the sun so trying to human beings at midday. But my mother was enchanted with this row, so perfectly new to her, and the negro boat-songs also delighted her. There were six splendid oarsmen, who sang from the moment the boat got well under way. Oh, there is nothing like the rhythm and swing of those boat-songs. "In case if I neber see you any mo', I'm hopes to meet yu on Canaan's happy sho'," and "Roll, Jordan, Roll," and "Run, Mary, Run," "Drinkin' Wine, Drinkin' Wine," "Oh, Zion!" I am filled with longing when I think of them. I was born at the seaside, and from that time until I was eighteen, the move from the plantation to the sea beach at the end of May, and the return home to the plantation the first week

[69]

in November were great events and a perfect joy.

Of course, it was different for my mother, for the tearing up of stakes just as she had got accustomed to her new home and new life, the packing up of everything necessary for comfort for every member of the household for the summer and autumn was terrific. It required so much thought, so many lists, so much actual labor. At the same time carpets, curtains, and all the winter clothing had to be aired, sunned, and put up with camphor against the moths. She was pretty well worn out and tired by this new aspect of her future life, this upheaval and earthquake to be gone through twice a year, so that when she stepped into the boat she was not her gayest self; but, when the things were all stored in, the lunch-baskets and valises and a big moss-wrapped bunch of roses, and the dogs at her feet; when papa, seated by her, took the rudder ropes, when the boat shot out into the river and the hands broke into song, preceded by each one calling aloud to the other, "Let's go, boys, let's go," she told me it was the most delightful revelation and sensation of her life almost. She had never been in a rowboat before; she had never been on a river. She had grown up in the interior, far in the hill country near the upper waters of the Savannah River, a rocky stream, where no woman ever thought of going in a boat. This swift, delightful movement, with the glorious sunshine and fresh morning breeze — for they always made an early start, there being so much to be done at the other end — made the row only too short.

But new pleasures awaited her, for the flat with the horses had gone ahead of them, starting with the ebb tide, at four in the morning; and, when they landed at the wharf at Waverly on the Waccamaw (which belonged to my father's elder brother, General Joseph Allston, who died leaving his two sons, Joseph Blythe and William Allan, to papa's care and guardianship), they found the horses all ready saddled, and they mounted and rode the four miles to "Canaan," where they were to spend the summer. It was on the seashore, just at an inlet where the ocean view was; and, as mamma saw the great waves come rolling in, she was filled with joy anew. To me it has always been intoxicating, that first view each year of the waves rolling, rolling; and the smell of the sea, and the brilliant blue expanse; but then I was born there and it is like a renewal of birth.

My mother enjoyed her life here. It was much simpler than that at the plantation, with fewer servants, and that she much enjoyed. They had breakfast at six o'clock every morning, and as soon as breakfast was over, papa mounted his horse and rode to Waverly, where the boat met him. His horse was put in the stable and he rowed to Chicora, went over all the crop, the rice-fields first, landing on the bank opposite the house and walking round all the planted fields, seeing that the water was kept on the rice just at the right depth, that the fields which had been dried for hoeing were dry enough to begin on them with the hoe. There is a real science in rice-planting, and my father was thoroughly versed in it and most diligent in seeing after the treatment of each field. He was always followed by the trunk minder, Jacob, and in every field Jacob went down the bank to the water edge and drew out a stalk or two of rice for papa to examine the root growth, by which the water is managed. This accomplished, papa crossed to the house, where a horse was ready saddled. He mounted and rode all over the upland crop, corn, potatoes, oats, peas; went into the house, which Maum Mary kept fresh and clean, wrote a few letters, drank a glass of buttermilk and ate some fruit, got into his boat again, and returned to the seashore for a three-o'clock dinner, having done a tremendous day's work; and he never failed, with all his work, to go into the garden and gather a bunch of roses and pink oleander to bring to mamma. Of course, his homecoming was the event of the day to my mother.

Soon papa's aunt, Mrs. Blythe, came to be with them for the summer, which was a great pleasure to mamma. She was a woman of noble character and ample means, who was specially devoted to my father, having no children of her own, and recognizing in him a kindred nature. Aunt Blythe was a true specimen of the "grande dame" of the old South. She had been brought up to responsibility, to command herself and others; she was an old lady when mamma first knew her, but tall and stately in figure and beautiful in face. She brought her own barouche, horses, and coachman and footman, and her own maid and laundress — in short, a retinue. I never saw Aunt Blythe, as she died before I was born, but the tales of her generosity and her grandeur which were told by white and black placed her in the category of fairies and other benign spirits. I was named after Aunt Blythe, a rare instance of posthumous gratitude, I think; and my mother, in the way she did it, showed a sympathetic, romantic understanding of Aunt Blythe's nature. She had been sought in marriage in her early youth by her first cousin, John Waties; but, when he approached her father and asked for his consent, he refused absolutely, as he disapproved of the marriage of cousins. So Aunt Blythe and her lover agreed not to be married during the father's lifetime. Alas, alas! John Waties died very soon! He left all his property to his fiancée, which made her the rich woman of the family. This property included a large and valuable rice-plantation, with a large number of negroes. Aunt Blythe felt this a great trust and responsibility and most difficult to manage, for it was almost impossible to get an overseer who would treat the negroes with gentleness and justice. The men who sought the place of overseer in those days were invariably from the North, their one idea being to get as much work from the hands as possible, and, consequently, make as much money. Aunt Blythe could not live alone in this isolated spot, the barony of Friendfield (it is the plantation now owned by Doctor Baruch and kept by

him as a game-preserve), and, after trying one
overseer after another, and finding them cruel and
regardless in their treatment of her people, she
accepted one of her many suitors, Doctor Blythe,
who had been a surgeon in the Revolutionary
War. She was then able to live on her plantation and to see that her negroes were kindly and
properly managed and looked after. Mamma became devoted to Aunt Blythe and wanted to
name her second daughter after her, but my
father wanted her named after his mother, who
had died a few years before his marriage, so he
named her Charlotte; but mamma wanted Aunt
Blythe's name in, so she asked to have the name
Charlotte Frances — Aunt Blythe's name was
Elizabeth Frances — and papa consented, but he
always called the beautiful little girl Charlotte,
while mamma called her Frances. She died when
she was about four, a grief my mother felt to the
very end, with strange poignancy. When, some
years after Aunt Blythe's death, I made my appearance on the scene, mamma named me for her;
but, instead of giving me the very pretty name
of her excellent husband, she gave me the name
of the man she loved, John Waties. So, instead
of being Elizabeth Blythe Allston, I was named

Elizabeth Waties Allston; not nearly so pretty a name, but it really made me the child of romance, I think. It was a beautiful thought and would have greatly pleased Aunt Blythe if she had known.

All of this has taken me from that first summer of my mother's married life on the seashore. It was a very happy one, the long mornings spent in sewing and talking with one who knew people and life, which my mother did not at all; and, above all, who knew this very peculiar life, surrounded by hundreds of a different race, with absolutely different characteristics and ideas. Mamma told me that once she had said in a despairing voice to her:

"But, auntie, are there no honest negroes? In your experience, have you found none honest?"

" My dear, I have found none honest, but I have found many, many trustworthy; and, Adèle, when you think of it, that really is a higher quality. It is like bravery and courage; bravery is the natural, physical almost, absence of fear; courage is the spiritual quality which makes a man encounter danger confidently in spite of inward fear. And so honesty is a natural endowment, but trustworthiness is the quality of loyalty, of fidelity which will make a man die rather than betray a trust; and that beautiful quality I have often found. When found, you must give it full recognition and seem to trust absolutely; one trace of suspicion will kill it; but one may make a mistake, and it is well, with every appearance of complete trust, to keep your mind alert and on the subject."

My mother exclaimed: "Oh, my dear auntie, I do not see how I can live my whole life amid these people! I don't see how you have done it and kept your beautiful poise and serenity! To be always among people whom I do not understand and whom I must guide and teach and lead on like children! It frightens me!"

Aunt Blythe laid her hand on my mother's hand and said: "Adèle, it is a life of self-repression and effort, but it is far from being a degrading life, as you have once said to me. It is a very noble life, if a woman does her full duty in it. It is the life of a missionary, really; one must teach, train, uplift, encourage — always encourage, even in reproof. I grant you it is a life of effort; but, my child, it is *our life*: the life of those who have the great responsibility of owning human beings. We are responsible before our Maker for not only their bodies, but their souls; and never must we for one moment forget that. To be the wife of a rice-planter is no place for a pleasure-loving, indolent woman, but for an earnest, true-hearted woman it is a great opportunity, a great education. To train others one must first train oneself; it requires method, power of organization, grasp of detail, perception of character, power of speech; above all, endless self-control. That is why I pleaded with my dear sister until she consented to send Robert to West Point instead of to college. Robert was to be a manager and owner of large estates and many negroes. He was a high-spirited, high-tempered boy, brought up principally by women. The discipline of four years at West Point would teach him first of all to obey, to yield promptly to authority; and no one can command unless he has first learned to obey. It rejoices my heart to see Robert the strong, absolutely self-controlled, self-contained man he now is; for I mean to leave him my property and my negroes, to whom I have devoted much care, and who are now far above the average in every way, and I know he will continue my work; and, from what I see of you, my child, I believe you will help him."

My mother told me that this talk with Aunt

Blythe influenced her whole life. It altered completely her point of view. It enabled her to see a light on the path ahead of her, where all had been dark and stormy before; the life which had looked to her unbearable, and to her mind almost degrading. Aunt Blythe urged her daily to organize her household so that she would have less physical work herself, and that part should be delegated to the servants, who might not at first do it well, but who could be taught and trained to do it regularly and in the end well. With Aunt Blythe's help she arranged a programme of duties for each servant, and Aunt Blythe's trained and very superior maid was able to assist greatly in the training of mamma's willing but raw servants.

The old lady was most regular in taking her daily drives and always insisted on my mother's going with her. It was a great amusement to her to see the preparations made. Aunt Blythe was big and heavy and always wore black satin slippers without heels. Mamma said she had never seen her take a step on mother earth except to and from the carriage, when she was always assisted. She wore an ample, plainly gathered black silk gown, with waist attached to skirt, cut rather low in the neck, and a white kerchief of fine white net for morning, and lace for dress, crossed in front, and a white cap. We have her portrait by Sully in that dress. She always carried a large silk bag filled with useful things, and as they met darkies on the way, Aunt Blythe would throw out to each one, without stopping the carriage, a handkerchief or apron, a paper of needles, or a paper of pins, or a spool of thread, or a card of buttons or hooks and eyes, or a spoon or fork — all things greatly prized, for in those days all these things were much scarcer than they are to-day, and there were no country shops as there are now, and, consequently, such small things were worth ten times as much as now to people, though they might not really cost as much as they now do. Sometimes it was a little package of tea or coffee or sugar which she had Minda, her maid, prepare and tie up securely for the purpose. Naturally, "Miss Betsey Bly" was looked upon as a great personage, and her path in her daily drives was apt to be crossed by many foot-passengers, who greeted her with profound courtesies, and apron skilfully tucked over the arm, so that it could be extended in time to receive anything.

CHAPTER VIII

FIRST CHILD—PLANTATION LIFE

THE next winter, in February, mamma's first child, a son, named Benjamin, after papa's father, was born. She was desperately ill, and her beautiful hair was cut as short as possible. Papa had thought it wisest for her to accede to her brother and his wife's urgent request that she should go to them in Charleston for the event; and it was most fortunate, for had she been taken ill at home, with a doctor far away, she probably would not have lived. As it was, her recovery was slow, and it was some time before she could resume her normal life at home. Aunt May, her unmarried sister, went home with her when she returned, and stayed until she regained her usual health. Aunt May was the only plain sister, for although she had beautiful complexion, brown hair, and fine figure, her face was not pretty, — but she made up in wit what she lacked in beauty. She was the wittiest, most amusing companion, and had great domestic gifts as housekeeper. Aunt May's coffee, Aunt May's rolls and bread, in short, every article on her table was superior, and, of course, this was a great comfort to mamma. There was only one drawback. Aunt May had no patience with incompetence, and the servants were a terrible trial to her, and mamma had to hear hourly of their shortcomings, which she knew only too well already, and to sympathize with Aunt May over them.

My mother spent a very anxious time in the first year of her eldest child's life. He was very delicate, and mamma knew nothing about babies. The plantation nurses seemed to her very ignorant, and she was afraid to trust the baby to them. However, any one who has read Doctor Sims's very interesting account of his early practice, especially among babies, well knows that these nurses, many of them, had learned through the constant care of babies how to manage them in a way surprising to one whose knowledge is altogether theoretic and scientific. Anyway, my brother grew and strengthened before the next baby came two years afterward. Robert was a very beautiful, strong child, and from the first gave no anxiety or trouble, only delight to mamma; and the little boys were always taken for twins, the elder being small for his age and the younger large.

Two years passed, and another baby came. This was the first little girl, and papa wished to name her for his mother, Charlotte Ann, and mamma asked that part of Aunt Blythe's name be added — her name was Elizabeth Frances. She had died the winter before, and mamma missed her dreadfully. So the little girl was called Charlotte Frances; and, in the household with its number of servants, you could always distinguish those devoted to my mother, who always spoke of "Miss Fanny," and those devoted to my father, who spoke of "Miss Cha'lot." But I never knew this from mamma, and do not know if it were so. Hearing of her only from mamma, I only knew of her as Fanny, my perfectly beautiful little sister.

Of these years I know very little, nothing, indeed, except that my parents went the summer following to Newport and New York, and visited papa's uncle, the great painter, Washington Allston, in Boston. When Mr. Flagg was looking over the great man's letters preparatory to publishing his life and letters, he found one from Washington Allston to his mother, speaking of this visit and of my mother's beauty and charm; and Mr. Flagg very kindly sent this letter to my mother, who gave it to me, and there is quite a contest among my nieces and nephews as to who will be the lucky one to whom I leave it. Mamma was greatly impressed by the ethereal beauty of the artist. She had at this time as nurse for the baby a woman from the State of New York, who took the little one in to see and be seen by her great-uncle. When she came out of the studio she said to mamma: "Surely, your uncle has the face of an angel, ma'am."

Three years passed, mamma very happy with her little family of interesting children, two of them so beautiful that wherever they went the nurse was stopped on the street by those who remarked on the wonderful beauty of Robert and Fanny. Poor, dear little Ben was neither beautiful nor strong, but he had a good mind and powerful will. Mamma often went to Charleston to visit her brother and sisters there, for by this time the youngest sister, Harriet, was also married to a young and very clever lawyer, Henry Deas Lesesne, who was in the law office of James L. Petigru, and she had her charming home in Charleston; so there were three homes to be visited there. Aunt Louise had relented in her attitude to my father and was always hospitably anxious to entertain the little family. Aunt Blythe had left her fortune to my father and the two boys, still babies though they were, to the surprise and indignation of many. So these were happy prosperous years.

Papa found the house at Chicora too small for the growing family, and began the planning of a new one, to which the two very large down-stairs rooms of the old one should be attached as an L. As the spring came on, a new baby was expected, and mamma hoped it would be a little girl, to name after her mother. As my mother dreaded the move to the sea, which involved so much troublesome packing, my father built a summer house, what would now be called a bungalow, for it had large, airy rooms, but all on one floor, at a pineland about eight miles north of the plantation on the same side of the Pedee, where he had a large tract of land, and where the cattle went always in summer. It was called "The Meadows." Mamma was very pleased to be so near the plantation, for she could drive down in the afternoons and see after her flower-garden, which was beautiful and her delight. She gathered great baskets of roses and brought them back. The Meadows was very prettily situated in a savannah, which was a natural garden of wild flowers — great, brilliant tiger-lilies, white and yellow orchis, the pink deer-grass, with its sweet leaf, pink saltatia, as well as white, and ferns everywhere.

Here, in this isolated new summer home, miles away from any neighbor, mamma was taken ill about two months before the time set for the baby's coming. Hastily the doctor was summoned, a very young man, still unmarried, but one who showed early his skill and proficiency as a family doctor; then the monthly nurse, as it was then called, Mary Holland, was found and brought. Fortunately, she had been employed in Georgetown and had not yet returned to Charleston, where she lived, and was in great demand by the doctors of best standing. I remember her as an old woman, but still tall and stately in figure, and with great dignity and poise. She was about the color of an Indian. It was a mercy she could be got, for my mother was desperately ill; but the little girl so hoped for was born, and my mother did not die. When she became strong enough to speak, and my father was with her, she said: "I want to see little Louise."

My father answered: "I will bring little Adèle to you myself."

She exclaimed: "Oh, Mr. Allston, I do not

want the baby named after me! I must name her for my dear mother."

But he answered: "I wish her to bear the name of my beloved wife."

She said nothing, but the tears which all of her suffering had not brought, now rolled down her cheeks. In a little while papa returned with the small bundle of flannel wrappings and most skilfully and tenderly unfolded them until the baby was visible.

Mamma looked at her, and then with something of her wonted spirit said: "You may call her Adèle if you like! Poor little soul, she cannot live! Take her away!"

I must think that this exhibition of almost cruel obstinacy on my father's part was due to the fact that the doctor had told him mamma could not possibly recover, and he thought it the only chance to have a little girl to name after her.

Wonderful tales were told of the smallness of the little Adèle. "She was put into a quart cup with ease and comfort to her." After mamma was well enough to hold her and play with her, she passed her wedding-ring over her hand and on her arm as a bracelet! But the little Adèle had a grit and grip on life which astounded every one, and she grew to womanhood, a beautiful creature in face, form, and spirit. She married and had seven children, and never lost one from illness. They grew up healthy and strong. The tiny Adèle was born August 16, 1840, in the very middle of a very hot summer. Of course, my mother's return to health was slow and tedious.

One can cast one's mind back to that date, when ice was so great a luxury that it was only to be had in the North, where it was cut and put up in the winter. The Meadows was twenty miles from the nearest town and post-office, Georgetown, and everything had to be brought up by the plantation wagons and team. But milk and butter and cream were abundant, also poultry and eggs; and the Pedee furnished most delicious fish — bream and Virginia perch and trout. There were figs in abundance and also peaches, but the latter were small and a good deal troubled with cuculio. They were, however, very good stewed, and my mother made quantities of delicious preserves from them.

Around the house at Chicora grew luxuriant orangetrees, only the bitter-sweet; but these oranges make the nicest marmalade, so mamma put up quantities of that for winter use. Her vegetable-garden was always full of delicious things — cucumbers, tomatoes, eggplant, and okra; and, as my father killed beef and mutton every week for use on the plantation, she had the very best soups and steaks; and there were always wild ducks to be had.   Also, after August 1, there was venison in the house, for my father was devoted to deer-hunting.   At the time the negroes understood preserving the venison in the hottest weather by exposing it to the broiling sun.   I do not know what else they did, for it is now a lost art; but it was called "jerked venison" and was a delicious breakfast dish, when shaved very thin and broiled. They also preserved fish in the same way — called "corned fish" — it was a great breakfast dish broiled.   Besides all this, about the end of August the rice-birds began to swarm over the rice, sucking out all the grain when in the milk stage.   This necessitated the putting out of bird-minders in great numbers, who shot the little birds as they rose in clouds from the rice at the least noise. These rice-birds are the most delicious morsels; smaller than any other bird that is used for food, I think, so that a man with a good appetite can eat a dozen, and I, myself, have eaten six.   When they go out at the end of harvest, another delicious little bird comes in, called locally a coot, but really the rail or soarer of Maryland. All these things made living easy and abundant, for they came in great quantities.

Mamma spoke with great pleasure of this part of her life when she could thoroughly enjoy her little family, sorrow not yet having clouded her horizon. When the little Adèle was two years old came a little sister, strong, healthy, and beautiful, to bear the name of the beloved little French mother, Louise Gibert — then her cup of happiness was full. She had come to love the plantation life, with its duties and its power to help the sick, to have the girls taught to sew and cut out simple garments, to supply proper and plentiful nourishment for the hospital — all this came to be a joy to her. There was on the plantation, besides the hospital or "sick-house," a "children's house," where all the mothers who were going out to work brought their children to be cared for during the day. The nursing babies, who were always taken care of by a child of ten or eleven, were carried to the mothers at regular intervals to be nursed. The head nurse, old Maum Phibby (Phœbe), was a great personage, and an administrator, having two under her, a nurse and a cook. Maum Phibby trained the children big enough to learn, teaching them to run up a seam and hem, in the way of sewing, and to knit first squares for wash-cloths, and then stockings, and then to spin. When the war came there was not a grown woman on the plantation who could not knit stockings or spin yarn. Weaving was only taught to certain young women who showed ability and some mechanical skill.

Mamma walked out often to the sick-house to see the patients and taste the soup and other nourishment, and then on to the "chillun's house" to see how their food was prepared, and whether they were all kept clean and healthy. This she did all her life, and I remember the joy of being allowed to go with her and of seeing the children all lined up in rows, their black skins shining, as clean black skins do, in a delightful way, their white teeth gleaming as they dropped their courtesies as mamma passed, each one holding in her hand some piece of work to exhibit. They were a healthy, happy lot and very clean, as it was an important part of Maum Phibby's duties to report the mothers who were negligent of "clean linen." * There was in the children's

---

* It is one of the peculiarities of the darkies of the past that they always spoke of that innermost garment which Shakespeare calls "a shift" as "their linen," even if it was made of coarse, unbleached homespun.

house, as well as the sick-house, a tin tub, that in the hospital big enough for the tallest man to lie straight in, and that at the children's house smaller; and any number of huge black kettles, so that hot water in great quantities could be got very quickly on the open fires. The children were bathed and scrubbed once a week by Maum Phibby, and woe to the mother whose child was not found to have been kept clean in the meantime. I have two of those immense coffin-shaped tubs now, perfectly good and strong, and I had one freshly painted and used it until two years ago, when I was able to put in a modern bathtub. At the end of the war, when furniture and every portable thing was carried off by the darkies, the bath-tubs from the sick-house were the one thing not taken. They were conspicuously in poor repute, one thing that nobody wanted! The coffin-shaped tub has a great recommendation, as taking less than half the water to cover a person entirely than the modern tub, and a very hot bath could be quickly given.

Mamma every Sunday afternoon had all the children big enough to come assembled in the little church in the avenue, and taught them what she could of the great mercy of God and what he expected of his children. It was always spoken of as "katekism," and was the event of the week to the children — their best clothes, their cleanest faces, and oh, such smiling faces greeted mamma when she arrived at the church! After the lesson a big cake was brought in a wheelbarrow by one of the house-boys, convoyed by Maum Mary, who cut it with much ceremony, and each child went up to the barrow, dropped a courtesy and received a slice, then passed to my mother with another courtesy, filed out and scampered happily home as soon as safe from Maum Mary's paralyzing eye.

All her life mamma kept this up, and in later years we children were allowed to go on condition that we should sit still and listen to the catechism, and ask for no cake until every child had had his share. Then we were allowed a few scraps, which tasted nicer than any other cake.

CHAPTER IX

FIRST GRIEVING

ONE spring, when the little Louise was about three, I think, Adèle five, Fanny seven, Robert nine, Ben eleven, a neighbor wrote from Charleston to mamma, asking if she would receive her and her two children for a night. The children had been ill with scarlet fever, but were well again, and pronounced by the doctor fit to travel; but, in order to reach their home on Sandy Island in one day they would have to be out late in the evening; and she feared the night air, so took the liberty of begging mamma to receive them for the night. My mother wrote she would be happy to do so, and they came, spent the night, went on their way the next day. My mother had had no fear and the children played together. She felt as the doctor had pronounced them fit to travel it was perfectly safe. A few days after the visit Robert was playing, when he suddenly dropped his playthings and put his head in mamma's lap, saying he felt sick. It was the dread disease. His illness was terrible from the first, but very short. He died. Then Fanny took it and followed rapidly, though Robert had been isolated from the moment he was taken. My poor mother was prostrated with her passionate grief. Every precaution then known was taken in the way of fumigation and burning up bedding and clothing, and the plague was stayed.

A great longing to visit the home of her childhood seized my mother, and my father felt it was a great thing that she should have the desire to go, as he really feared for her mind and health. So when all possible danger of contagion was considered over, he took her and the three children who were left up to Abbeville to the farm called Badwell, where she was born, and where her beloved mother lay in the family burying-ground with the pasteur of the desert, Jean Louis Gibert, her father. My father left them there and returned to his work. In a few days the beautiful little Louise was taken ill and died, and was laid by her grandmother in the God's acre! I cannot bear to think of my mother's suffering at this time. The tragedy of it! The child named at last for her mother, on this much-longed-for visit to her mother's home. Now her three beautiful, strong children were gone, leaving only the delicate Ben and the delicate and tiny seven-months' child,

Adèle. It seems like the crushing out of some dainty, happy creature, a beautiful, full, happy life drained of its joy, leaving only stern, exacting duty!

I know my dear father suffered terribly at this time, too, but he never spoke to me of it. He never found it possible to put his deeper feelings into words. I think he and my mother were a great comfort to each other in their grief, and I think it was this summer that my father had the desperate illness of which my mother has told me, and I believe it was his return from the jaws of death which made her first feel life held a future for her.

They were in the same isolated, remote summer house, The Meadows. Papa came home from his harvest work on the plantation much exhausted, went at once to bed, and when mamma followed him at midnight she knew he was desperately ill — a burning, consuming fever, and his rapid whispered speech showed him delirious. She called the servants, wrote a note to Doctor Sparkman, asking him to come at once, telling him how suddenly papa had been taken, put a man on horseback and sent him off in the night, telling him to go from place to place until he found the doctor. Then

she proceeded to do what she could for the patient
to reduce the awful fever. Cloths wrung out in
water fresh from the spring on head and face and
hands was all she could do to cool it, as there was
no ice. Then she had a tub of hot water brought
and with the help of Hynes, the house-servant,
put his feet to the knees in that, covering him
with blankets to produce steam. Mercifully this
quieted him and the jabbering ceased and he slept.
Daylight came, no doctor, no sound came to her
listening ear of horse-hoofs. The heavy sleep as
of one drugged lasted until she was frightened,
but she feared to wake him. She looked after the
children, having Hynes, who was very faithful
and intelligent, to sit by papa and fan him. She
gave the children their breakfast and tried to eat,
herself, for she knew she would need all her
strength. Dinner-time came, evening, night. Oh,
the long hours, how they dragged! She thought
of her desperate, passionate grief for her children,
feeling she could not bear it. Had God heard
her rebellious murmurings, and was he going to
show her now how blessed she had then been,
having her husband left to her! How unutter-
ably worse this grief would be! How hopeless,
indeed, would life be without him!

And so the hours wore on, but she was not idle; she thought of everybody and did everything for the comfort of the house. Just at midnight the dogs began to bark. She went on the piazza and heard wheels approaching. She had kept the dinner-table laid with flowers and silver and candles, all bright and cheery. As soon as she heard wheels she ordered the servants to bring in dinner, and when the doctor entered and said, "How is Colonel Allston?" she said, "Doctor, sit down and dine first, and then I will take you in to see him." He sat down, and she went to the sick-room, where things were unchanged, the same drugged sleep and heavy breathing. As soon as the doctor had finished, he came and listened to her accurate account of all the symptoms. Then the fight began. I do not know what he gave or what he did, but he remained doing all that his skill and science suggested, for thirty-six hours, and then he felt for the first time that there was hope, and left to see after his other patients. He told my mother that he had been with a desperately ill patient on Santee, thirty miles south of his home, for twenty-four hours; when he returned to his home he found mamma's note and the servant, and without going into the house, though he was famished for food after a thirty-mile drive, he had had a fresh horse put in and came right on. Then he said: "Oh, Mrs. Allston, if every one thought of the doctor as you do, the life of a country doctor would be a different thing, and fewer of them would become dependent on stimulants. I was exhausted, but expected to see and prescribe for the patient before having food. When I saw that delicious dinner of roast duck and vegetables I was completely surprised, but I blessed you and felt how much clearer my brain, how much better my condition to prescribe for the patient, and how much better chance it gave him for life, though, I confess, when I first saw Colonel Allston I did not feel there was any chance of saving him." I tell all this just as my mother told it to me. It shows what a woman she was. My father recovered slowly, and it was the last summer they spent at The Meadows, the distance from all help in illness being too great.

The next May, 1845, they again moved to Canaan Seashore, where my mother had spent her first summer of married life. They went early in May and I was born on the 29th of that month. Naturally, I suppose, after all the sorrow and anxiety mamma had had, I was a miserably delicate, nervous baby, and I have heard mamma say that for months they were afraid to take me out of the house at all. At the end of that time the house which papa was building on Pawley's Island, just across the marsh and creek from Canaan, was finished, and they determined to move the household over to the island for the rest of the summer. That was my first outing, and the times I was taken out of the room afterward were few and far between, for it seems after going out I never closed my eyes at all that night. I was a poor sleeper at any time, but after going out I was no sleeper at all. The floor of my dear mother's room on the beach is seamed all over by the marks of the rocking-chair in which I was eternally rocked! They had a hard struggle to keep me alive. Both mamma and papa wanted me named for the dear old aunt who had been such a blessing to everybody, so I was named Elizabeth Waties, mamma with tender sympathy giving me the name she would have borne had her dream of love materialized. I seemed to be marked for sadness, with deep lines under my eyes, as though I had already wept much, which I certainly had, only with a baby it is not weeping, but crying, with the accompaniment of much noise.

The winter I was two years old, one Sunday mamma had gone with papa in a boat to All Saints' Church, seven miles away on the Waccamaw. She looked out of the window as she listened to dear, saintly Mr. Glennie's sermon, and across her vision passed a young man walking in the churchyard, holding by the hand little Ben, who had been allowed to go out when the sermon began. She was much excited, because she could not imagine what stranger could possibly be there. As he passed a second time she recognized her beloved brother Charles, whom she had not seen for several years. One can understand that the rest of Mr. Glennie's excellent discourse was lost to her, and she could scarcely wait for the blessing, to rush out and meet the stranger.

He was in the army, having graduated from West Point in 1829. He told her he was on his way to Florida, and had managed to arrange to spend one day with her, but it could only be one. So when he reached the plantation and found she had gone by water to church so far away, he ordered a boat, and followed her, so as to lose nothing of his time with her. This visit was the greatest joy to my mother. He was her youngest brother and her special favorite. She was distressed when he told her where he was going and why. The U. S. post at Tampa, Florida, had proved a very deadly one. One officer after another who had been sent there in command had contracted the terrible malarial fever of the country and died soon after getting there. His friend Ramsay had been ordered there, and he found him in despair one day, having just received his orders. He said he had a wife and a mother, both dependent on him, and it was awful to him to be going to certain death when he thought of them and what would become of them. Uncle Charles said at once: "Ramsay, I will take your place; if I apply for the exchange, I can get it, and I have no one dependent upon me, so I have the right to do it." The exchange had been effected and Uncle Charles was on his way to take the place which West Point for years sang of in their class song, "Benny Havens, Oh!" as "Tampa's deadly shore." Uncle Charles left early the next morning. By the time my next little brother came, a boy born the 31st of the next July, Uncle Charles had accomplished his sacrifice and fallen a victim to the fever, so the baby was named Charles Petigru; and everybody always loved him more than any of the other children. He was so beautiful

and so sweet and good that we all expected him
to die, but he didn't, but grew up to be a man
and always a blessing to all around him.

Mamma's grief at her brother's death was great,
but she had learned to suffer without rebellion,
and as some wise one has written, "there is great
peace and strength in an accepted sorrow." She
always felt very proud of the heroism and self-
sacrifice of Uncle Charles's death. "No greater
love is there than that a man give his life for his
friend"; that is not quoted exactly, but it sets a
man very high. Now we are living in such a
heroic time, with men giving their lives on the
battle-field to save one another, every hour, that
perhaps it does not seem as grand a thing. But
when one thinks of a very young, handsome, popular man deliberately giving up a choice army
post to take one which meant certain, unheroic,
painful, and obscure death, it seems to me very,
very heroic and beautiful. After Uncle Charles's
death — I think he was the seventh commanding
officer cf the Tampa post who died in quick suc-
cession — the post was given up. Wonderful to
say, now since the science of stamping out disease
has reached such a height, Tampa is a health re-
sort! and one wonders what was the cause of that

death-dealing miasma which made the place so
fatal. On our way to the Chicago Exposition,
having to be some hours in Atlanta, we visited
the military station there, and I met a Captain
Ramsay, who told me he was the son of the officer
whose life had been saved by my Uncle Charles
Petigru's generous heroism, and seemed quite excited to meet two nieces and three great-nieces of
the heroic young lieutenant to whom his family
owed so much.

PART III

MYSELF

CHAPTER X

BABY WOES

HAVING brought things up to this point by telling what I heard from my dear mother, who had a wonderful memory, as well as a most dramatic power of speech, I must try now to put down what I remember myself. Here and there a scene stands out, just a medallion, as it were, a bas-relief from the far past, with everything as distinct and clear-cut as possible.

The very first is a very mortifying one to recount; but, if I am to put down all I remember, as I have been urged to do, I must be frank and truthful, or it will have no value. This is the old story of our first Mother Eve in that beautiful garden of Eden, temptation, fall, punishment. My mother was ill on Pawley's Island, the beach. I must have been about three. The wife of the family doctor (who was, when we were on the beach, Doctor Hasel) had sent a plate of very beautiful peaches to my mother, and they had been put on the Sheraton sideboard in the dining-room. They were so big that one could rest on a tumbler without going in, quite different from the ordinary peaches we had; indeed, I had never seen such peaches, as big as an orange they were and with bright-red cheeks. I gazed and gazed, walking through the room several times slowly. My father was sitting in the corner of the room at his desk, writing, with his back turned, and finally Satan prevailed and I tipped in softly with my little bare feet, and tried to reach the peaches; failing, I got a chair and put it alongside the sideboard, climbed up, got the top peach and quickly and quietly made my way into the thick shrubbery outside, and ate my beautiful and delicious capture with great delight. I was somewhat sticky and messy, but fortune favored me and I made my way into the nursery without meeting any one, washed my hands and face to the best of my ability, and then went in the corner of the piazza where my dolls were, and felt serenely happy. When I came out with my doll for a walk I found quite an excitement. First May, the Irish nurse who was head of the nursery, met me and asked if I had taken one of the beautiful peaches. Quite calmly I answered "No." Then every one I met told of the rape of the peach and asked if I knew anything about it. I always managed to answer in the same calm negative, though by this time I was far from feeling calm within. Finally May went to my father with many lamentations, and announced that one of the servants had taken one of the beautiful peaches from the sideboard. Papa said: "Send Miss Bessie to me." So I came and papa repeated the terrible question, as it had now come to be, and I answered with the same "No," but very faint was it this time, for I felt it was no use, as papa seemed to me to have all the qualities of the Deity, omniscience being one. He said with a terribly pained voice:

"My little daughter, why tell a lie? I was writing here and heard your little feet coming and going through the room, but thought of no possible harm until this outcry about the missing peach was brought to me, and then I turned and saw the chair placed by the sideboard, and knew what the little feet had been busy about, and sent for my little girl, feeling sure she would tell me what she had done. It was a shock to me to hear that 'No,' and a real grief. That my little daughter, named after my blessed Aunt Blythe, who was the soul of honor, should have taken one of the beautiful peaches sent to her mother who is ill, without asking for it, is bad enough; but that

that same little daughter should tell a lie about it is a great distress. But most of all is the fact that she told a lie which would leave the guilt to fall upon an innocent person! That is a terrible thing to have done, and I must punish you, so that you may never fall so low again. Go into the little room and wait until I come."

I went. The little room was a shed-room on the northeast corner of the piazza, which was kept always ready for any stray man guest who might arrive unexpectedly. The little mahogany bed was always made up with fresh sheets and white coverlet and looked very inviting. I sat in the rocking-chair and rocked, trying to make believe to myself that I did not care and was not frightened. After a while my father came and gave me a severe switching. When he had finished he kissed me, put me on the bed, and threw a light linen coverlet over me, and I went to sleep. I slept a long time, for when I woke up it was nearly dark, and I felt like an angel in heaven — so happy and peaceful and, above all, filled with a kind of adoration for my father. It is strange what a realization of right and wrong that gave me, baby though I was. I have never ceased to feel grateful to papa for the severity of that punishment. It *had* to be remembered, and it meant the holding aloft of honesty and truth, and the trampling in the dust of dishonesty and falsehood. No child is too young to have these basic principles taught them.

The next silhouette which stands out vividly is different. We had had the delight of a little sister added to our nursery. She was born in December, the only winter baby. All the rest of us were born in summer. I only remember the wild excitement in the nursery when May came in the early morning and announced, "You have a little sister," and how we scrambled out of bed and into our clothes hastily, hoping to see her. Of course, we did not have that joy for some days.

Then a long blank, only two years, really. It was summer. We were on Pawley's Island, and my father and mother had gone to New York, leaving us at home with the governess and nurse. Letters came saying that my mother was very ill, and instead of the carriage being ordered to meet her at the boat, directions came for a mattress to be placed in the wagon, and that was to meet her at Waverly. The afternoon came and we were so wild with expectation and excitement that the governess and nurse thought best to take us

across the causeway into the woods, with the bait
held out of meeting mamma as she came.

The walk in the woods was always a treat, so
we went joyfully — Della, who was twelve, and
Charley, the baby, still in her nurse's arms most
of the time, and myself. I remember principally
in this walk a spider, the biggest I ever saw until
I was an old woman. I was hanging on an oak
limb, quite near to the ground. It was rotten,
and it broke and I fell to the earth, and with me
fell out of the hollow limb a spider as big as a
dollar. I was terribly frightened and screamed
for a long time.

Soon after I was quieted we heard the rumble
of wheels, and the wagon came in sight, going
very slowly. As it came nearer we rushed forward to meet it, but papa, who rode on horseback beside it, held up his finger in warning, and
then placed it on his lips, so we remained quite
still until the wagon, in which we could see nothing, passed. Papa stopped behind, got down
from his horse and kissed us all, putting Charley
upon the horse, while he walked beside. He told
us that mamma was very ill, and we must be very
good and make no noise, but keep the house very
quiet. Della asked if we could see her and just

kiss her, but he said no; we must be content to know she had got safely home, and thank God for that, but we would not be able to see her until she was better. Then he mounted and rode on and caught up with the wagon. When the little procession of disappointed children reached the house my mother had been carried into her own room and put to bed. A nurse had arrived in the buggy and took charge of her room. The governess and May were told to keep us entirely in the western part of the house, where we could not be heard unless we made some outrageous noise.

This dear old house consisted of *two* houses, each with two immense rooms down-stairs with very high ceilings and many windows and doors, and two rooms above equally large, but only half stories. These two houses were placed at right angles; the front one, toward the beach, ran north and south, the other, toward the marsh, ran east and west. Both had wide piazzas around them, which made a large, cool, shady hall where they came together. Our nursery was in the northeast up-stairs room in the front house, and though it was over the dining-room and not over mamma's room, it was thought best to move us to the other side of the house entirely. So we slept in the bedroom next to the day-nursery, where we took our meals, at the extreme west of the house.

I cannot tell how long this stillness lasted, but it seems an age, as I look back. Then one day May came in and said mamma was better, and we had a new little brother, but we must still be very good and make no noise. I remember going very softly with my bare feet, holding Charley's hand, until we got to the piazza outside of mamma's room and waiting until we heard the baby cry. Then we knew the good news was true, and we crept back in delight to the playroom. Every day we made this trip, and for some days were rewarded by the delightful sound of the baby's voice; and then one day, though we sat a long time, there was no sound — all was still. And that day, after dinner, papa came in and told us the little brother had left us; God had taken him back to heaven.

We went out for our afternoon walk very solemnly, and as we walked I held tightly to Hagar's hand and said how I wished I could just once have seen my little brother. Hagar, who was a negro girl about fifteen, Maum 'Ria's daughter, and was assistant in the nursery, and went out to walk with us, said: "If yu didn't bin so coward,

I cud 'a show yu de baby, but yuse too cry-baby
en yu'll tell en git me in trubble." I declared I
would not cry and I would not tell, if only she
would let me see the little brother. Then she
told me that when she began to take water up
into the rooms, I must sit on the stairs and wait
till she beckoned to me, and then very softly I
must follow her up-stairs — all of which programme was carried out. And when we got into
the room above my mother's, she put me out of
the window on to the shed, and followed herself,
and we walked stealthily on the shingles, so they
would not creak, across the shed of the piazza to
the window of the other house, where the company
room was. The venetian was closed, but Hagar
put her hand between the slats and pulled the
bolt and opened the shutter and put me in, following, herself, quickly. There, on the white-cur-
tained dressing-table was a pretty white box of a
strange shape to me. Hagar lifted the white muslin which covered it and held me up so that I
could look in, and there was the most beautiful
doll I had ever seen. I looked with delight. I
can remember the little waxen face now. All
would have gone well if I had not suddenly stooped
and, before Hagar could stop me, kissed the lovely

thing. The awful cold of death sent such a shock
through me that I opened my mouth to scream,
but before any sound came Hagar clapped her
hand over my mouth and hissed into my ear:
"Ain't I say so! Yuse too cry-baby! I wish to
de Lawd I neber bring yu! Yu'll sho' tell en
git me in trubble!" I stifled my screams and
choked back my tears, Hagar shaming me and
adjuring me to silence until I was quiet enough
for us to attempt the perilous return trip. That
night I could not sleep. I sobbed and sobbed and
tossed on my little bed; the cold of that kiss
seemed to freeze me all over. May went to papa,
saying she feared I was going to be ill. He came
to the nursery at once, talked to me and patted
me and, when I only cried the more, he took me
in his arms and walked up and down the nursery,
singing to me. As the sobs still continued, he
asked: "What ails my little daughter; has she
any pain?"

"No."

"Has anything scared my little Bessie?"

Violently I shook my head and tried my best to
stop the sobs. I must keep my promise to Hagar.
But it was far into the night before my father's
sweet voice, singing hymn after hymn, soothed

me and the sense of safety in his strong arms brought quiet, and I slept, and he laid me gently in my little trundle-bed.

I remember nothing after that until one afternoon — I do not know if it was that summer or the next — we were going out for our usual walk on the beach, May with the little Louise in her arms, Charley trudging behind, I bringing up the rear. As we came round the piazza and were about to go down the front steps, papa, who was at his desk writing in the dining-room, called to May: "Mary, do not take the children farther than the Opening. We are going to have a storm and it will surely break when the tide changes." She came out and told us what papa had said.

I flung myself down on the top step and said: "If I can't go any farther than the Opening, I won't go at all."

May argued, she pleaded with me, she warned: "For the Lord's sake, child, don't let your father hear you! Come on then" — and she took my hand.

But at this I lay flat back on the piazza and yelled and shrieked: "If I can't go beyond the Opening, I won't go at all."

At last my father's voice came, calm and serene,

from the dining-room: "Never mind, Mary, leave her. Don't let the other children lose their walk. Go on to the beach." And she went.

I screamed louder and louder and kicked until my poor heels were all bruised, but I didn't care. The devil of temper had me in its clutches, and I was crazed by it. Finally papa came out and took me into the little Prophet's Chamber, and gave me a severe whipping. As before, I went to sleep on the little white bed and woke up feeling like an angel in heaven, with adoration in my heart for the God who had conquered the evil spirit which had possessed me. I always feel grateful for that first conquest of the evil spirit within me. It has, no doubt, saved me much suffering; but this poor, intense, self-willed nature has all its long life dashed itself against stone walls, crying: "All — or nothing!" And God has tried gently to win me to yield to his will, his plans, and I have rebelled. And he had to take from me all that he had given me with a free hand, as though I were his favorite child.

Never was a girl more blessed than I in her marriage, too happy to live, I often felt. Alas, my happiness so possessed me that it made me blind to the world outside. What cared I for the world, or outer world, as long as my little paradise was untouched? Alas, it had to go; and so one thing after another had to be taken before this poor piece of humanity was fit for the Master's use, able to yield and to help others to yield. And now I thank the great Father for all that crushing and sorrow, as I used as a little child to thank and adore my father for his punishments. There were only these two that I have told of. Never afterward did my father have to give me even a stern look. It was my joy and pride to win his approval, generally only a smile, but it meant more to me than the most lavish praise from any one else.

My father thought riding a most healthful exercise. My sister was a fearless horsewoman, and during the summers which we passed on this beautiful island, which had a splendid hard, broad beach three miles long, she spent all her afternoons on horseback. When she came home and dismounted, my father always put me on for a little ride. I was terribly afraid and it was a fearful joy to me. I nearly always cried when I was put on the horse, whose name was Typee; I would say: "Papa, I could canter all day, but it is the stopping I mind." I still remember with terror the high, hard trot which Typee found necessary in stopping; he could not go from his easy canter to his nice, easy walk without introducing this tremendous hard trot between, and when I was thrown up into the air I never knew whether I would drop back in the saddle or down on the sand. My brother Charley, two years younger, was a good and fearless rider; his horse Lady was swift and spirited, had a very easy gait and was not at all vicious, but nothing would induce me to mount her.

One day, when my father returned from a visit to the upper part of the State, he called me and said: "My little Bessie, I have brought a pony to be all your own; his name is Rabbit and he is very gentle, so that now you need not be afraid to ride, and you can go with Adèle instead of waiting until she comes home, for your ride."

Of course I appeared overjoyed and thanked him with enthusiasm, but in my heart I was terribly dismayed; go to ride with Della, who went fast all the time! No, indeed, I could not do that, but after Rabbit arrived, a little, dark-brown horse with kind eyes and slow ways, I was put on his back, weeping, every afternoon, and started off with Della; but Typee went so fast that I

begged her to go on and leave Rabbit and me to
our own devices, which she always did, so we
ambled along comfortably, he having a very nice
pace which suited me better than a canter or a
gallop. Della took her long, rapid ride and, returning, picked me up, so we came home demurely
together. It was supposed that I was becoming a
great horsewoman, and I really was getting over
my fear and ceased to weep as I was mounted.
Those quiet rambles along the beautiful, smooth
beach, where nothing could hurt you, — with the
great, beautiful sea, rolling in with its dashing
waves just beside me, but limited by its great
Creator — very soon became the greatest delight
and joy to me. I loved to be alone with this
wonderful companion, and would ride along about
a mile and then turn and come slowly back, so
that Della could reach me before we got home.
This conduct of my father's toward me showed his
wonderful insight, and the thought he gave each
individuality. Every one, my mother included,
feared the effect on me of forcing me to mount and
ride daily, when it was such pain to me, but he saw
that if that nervous fear of everything was recognized and encouraged, the rest of me would never
develop. Charley went to ride every morning with

a negro boy a few years older than himself, to see that he was not too rash. I doubt whether Brutus could be called a modifier, but he understood all about horses and was a good rider, teaching Charley a great deal, running races, and jumping ditches.

CHAPTER XI

THE LITTLE SCHOOLHOUSE — BOARDING-SCHOOL

THESE tragic memories all have as a background our summer home on Pawley's Island, which we always spoke of as "the beach," as though this were the only beach in the world. My next memories are of the little schoolhouse at Chicora and our two English governesses — Miss Wells, who was our first, I do not remember distinctly, but Miss Ayme, who stayed with us until I went to boarding-school at nine, plays a great part in my pictures of the early days.

My father had a two-roomed cottage about 300 yards from the house, in a sunny spot in the park, near the river. It was a beautiful situation, and each room had a fireplace, where we kept up splendid oakwood fires, and to this charming schoolhouse we went at nine and remained until two, having our lunch sent down to us there, and only returning to the house when the bell sounded for preparation for dinner. In this way we avoided the inevitable interruptions when the neighbors came to visit, for as they came from a dis-

tance of several miles always, it was quite a prolonged affair, meaning tea and bread-and-butter,
handed by Nelson on the big silver waiter, and
wine, handed by the footman on a smaller silver
waiter, and a great deal of talk. If we had been
in the house when we were called for, it would
have been impossible to refuse to send for us; but
the fact that we were at the "schoolhouse," which
could not be seen from the front door or piazza,
resulted in our never being summoned.

Miss Ayme was much before her day in many
things, especially in her insistence on physical
exercises, so in 1850 she introduced what is now
essential in all schools, calisthenics. We exercised with poles and dumb-bells, and my sister,
who stooped a little, was made to lie on her back
a certain length of time every day on a wide
plank, which was inclined at an angle, while Miss
Ayme read aloud to her: the result was seen all
her life in a beautiful figure, and erect, graceful
bearing. I walked up and down for an allotted
time each day, with a backboard, but as I had
gone to boarding-school when the time came that
I should have had the slanting-board treatment,
I never have acquired the beautiful carriage of
my sister. Miss Ayme also believed in telling

children many of the truths of nature, which at that time was considered very indiscreet if not immoral. She was a very good teacher and, besides being a good Christian, was a lady. She had queer little ways and was a never-ending amusement to our neighbors, who had not the appreciation of the higher standards and the vision of my father and mother. Her odd dress and very English speech struck them as her principal characteristics. Miss Ayme had been a governess in a family of the nobility in England. I have, I am sorry to say, forgotten the name, of which we used to get very tired, for she told many stories about the children, who seemed preternaturally good and were fed, to our minds, very poorly, principally on porridge, which sounded miserable to us. They were eager always for the top of Miss Ayme's boiled egg, which at that time in England was skilfully cut off with a knife, and she gave it to each one in turn, which they considered most generous of her.

When my sister was thirteen it was thought best by my parents to send her to boarding-school. There was one in Charleston, kept by Madame Togno, who took only a limited number, where French was the language spoken. This pleased my mother especially, and as the course of study was said to be very good, my sister was sent to Charleston in the early autumn. This left me as the only pupil for Miss Ayme, Charley being only six, and as she was an expensive teacher my parents decided to do without her after the New Year. I remember how I missed my sister, how terribly lonely I was without her, and how wild with delight I was when she returned in June, having enjoyed her school experiences very much and having improved in health as well as everything else, especially music, to which my father was devoted. So it was decided, as I was eager to go, that I should go too when she returned to Madame Togno's select French school. I was only nine, small for my age and very thin and nervous, and when one thinks of it now, it seems to have been an awful risk. But I feel quite sure it was most judicious; the companionship of girls of my own age was very good. The regulated life and study I had had at home were excellent, but I was alone, with no minds of my own age to measure myself with. At school I entered a class of fourteen little girls of my own age, day-scholars, some of them exceptionally well-grounded, bright children; and it did me a world of good to find I had to work hard if I wanted to keep up.

One lovely curly-haired, blue-eyed child that looked like an angel and a kitten combined, and who had been taught by her father like a boy, Sara White, kept me always at the greatest strain in the arithmetic, history, and dictation classes. Sara was not only the best girl in the class, but the prettiest and the tiniest. Her long, golden curls and her preternaturally clean white apron were my greatest envy. She was the dearest little case of enlarged conscience I have ever met. One day in class I saw her crying quietly, the big tears dropping onto her slate, and I whisperingly asked what was the matter. She told me between suppressed sniffs that her mother had forbidden her to go into the yard without her hat; she wanted to cross the yard to wash her slate, but madame had forbidden any girl to go into the closet where the hats were hung until recess! What a plight! I, being always daring, proceeded skilfully to go after a book across the room. I quickly entered the closet and got the hat, and Sara made her trip across the yard. Dear little strong, pure soul! She has lived a heroic life, at one time nearly supporting her family in New York by her china-painting. Still dainty and sweet, with her true blue eyes and golden, snow-touched curly hair, she is one of my dearest friends.

I learned French rapidly, as it was the language required of the boarding-pupils. I quickly picked up enough French words to pass me on and I invented many others, so that I appeared to be speaking French fluently to the older girls, who were painfully following rules and phrase-books. The ingenuity with which I added French-sounding terminals to English words so as to create the impression that I was speaking French was a great amusement to madame, and I became a great favorite with her. I was a tiny child, small and thin, with deep circles under my big eyes, with an uncannily alert mind, but shy and morbid by nature; very nervous and easily thrown into violent paroxysms of weeping by reproof. Madame was quick to find out that I responded to praise by redoubled effort, but wilted under disapproval and rebuke, and she kept me near her a great deal, and encouraged me to narrate in my own original French lingo all that I saw and heard, so that I soon got over my homesickness and learned quickly, but was in a fair way to be badly spoiled. The dining-room not being very large, madame had a table made in the shape of a horseshoe. She sat at the middle of the curve on the outside of the table, and I sat just opposite her inside, and my mission was to amuse her as well as every one else at the table, so that I scarcely took time to eat enough to keep me going. The meals were always excellent, as madame prided herself on her table and looked carefully after the selection of food and the cooking.

There were about twenty boarding-pupils, most of them young ladies being "finished off," in which process madame took much pride. We boasted three beauties, who were always put in the front rank when we went to concerts or to the theatre. Victoria Jordan looked absolutely like the pictures of the ill-fated Marie Antoinette, when dressed for a party. She married the year after this and we were all distressed by her sad fate. She and her husband were blown up in a steamer on the Mississippi on their wedding-trip. Carrie Elliot came next, I think, but many thought Adèle Allston, my sister, was the loveliest. Carrie was my first love; she was seven years my senior and was not impatient of my devotion. She married a very charming man, a cousin, who became in time a bishop, greatly admired and beloved — Bishop Robert Elliot, of Texas.

My principal trouble was the constant fear of fire. Soon after I got to school there was a big fire not far off in the middle of the night, and I was waked by the ringing of the bells and the awful cries of "Fire!" I was terrified and, on getting up, the red glare which lit up the whole sky was awful. At that time the fire department was made up of volunteers and the engines were drawn entirely by man-power, an excited mob of black and white pulling on a tremendous loop of rope, running at full speed and yelling "Fire!" as they went. One afternoon when there was a fire near the Battery, and we were standing on the front step to see if we could get even a glimpse of it, as the engine passed, the impulse was too strong for me. I rushed out and took my place on the rope and ran down the street, pulling and madly yelling with the rest. The other girls who saw it were afraid to tell madame, seeming actually to fear capital punishment, and hoping that I would have the sense to come back, myself. So it was not until madame missed me in the study-hour and inquired where I was that the dreadful truth was revealed. To their great surprise, madame laughed heartily and sent the cook to the fire to bring me back. This was a great joy to the cook, as to visit a fire to them is what an opera-ticket is to us. She found me in the rabble, and, after due delay, when she was supposed to be looking for me, and in which she was really enjoying the rare treat of meeting all her friends and imagining tragedies if there were none to see, we returned home fast friends. She held me tightly by the hand and narrated volubly the difficulty she had in finding me and then in getting me to come, how "she almost had to take me up and tote me" — all of which was pure fiction. I stood a miserable prisoner at the bar, but not at all repentant, only prepared for the worst. Madame used her finest sarcasm on me.

"Well, mademoiselle, I did not know you had joined the fire-brigade! I am sorry to deprive them of so strong and competent a member; but your parents, in placing you in my care, did not mention that as one of the branches in which I was to have you instructed, and you will now retire to bed without supper and remain there until to-morrow morning. And the next time the fire-bells ring, instead of allowing you to go out on the step to see it, you will be locked up." So, sorrowfully, I went up to my little bed. But it was very good for me for, of course, I was exhausted; and the cook, whose interest had been aroused in me for the first time, brought me a particularly nice supper. She had to wake me, for I was sound asleep.

After the fire terror, my next trouble was the going to bed. My sister and I occupied a very nice but small room. She slept in a single mahogany four-poster, with a white valance around it, under which during the day my trundle-bed was rolled. I was always sent to bed at eight. The maid went up, lit the gas, and pulled the trundle-bed out and then left, returning in fifteen minutes to put out the gas. She was not of the friendly kind and I always jumped into bed as I heard her coming. The valance of the tall bed hung over a part of my bed, as, if it was pulled out all the way, the door could not open wide, and I always imagined a robber was hid under that valance! My sister did not come till nine, and I lay there in a cold sweat till she came, perfectly certain I heard the man breathing. I always asked her in a whisper in French to look under the bed, and, of course, the man not being there, I recovered and was asleep before she got in bed; but no one can imagine how I suffered from this foolish fright.

My music was another trial this first year. I had the crossest teacher that ever was. I cannot remember her name, for we only called her "mademoiselle," but she scolded me and cracked my knuckles till I cried, at every lesson. These were my only troubles, however, and I was very happy and dreamed many dreams. It was hard to find a place where one could dream in peace; there were girls everywhere jabbering bad French; but I found a delightful place — under the dining-table! I was a very morbid child with many imaginary sorrows, and it was a great relief to me to write journals and pour out my woes to these safe confidants. Every scrap of paper was secured and kept in my pocket, for at that day we had a large, capacious pocket in every frock, so that I had stores of paper, and when the outside world was too hard and unfeeling, I watched my chance when no one was near, and slipped to my quiet retreat under the big horseshoe dining-table, with its white cloth which swept the floor, and wrote and wrote until my griefs were assuaged, then rolled up my treasure and returned to the outer world refreshed. When the manuscript became too bulky I buried it in the garden under the pettis porum bushes. This I kept up for years, and in that way I buried my sorrows.

In the early spring mamma wrote to madame

and asked that she would select and buy our spring and summer things, sending her a liberal check for the purpose. This delighted madame, and she bought and had made for us clothes that I could not abide and refused to wear at first. A straw bonnet trimmed with blue ribbons and a curl of straw around the front is a nightmare to me still. It was just like an old lady's bonnet in the sixties, and tied under the chin; but, as soon as that was done the bonnet fell back off of my head, and in order to keep it on at all I had to keep my left hand clapped on the back. Then the frock was a purple-and-white delaine, stripes of purple flowers on a white ground. This was made with a full waist buttoned at the back, what was called "half high neck," and had a very full deep frill around it of cotton lace! Oh, how I hated it! And when we were dressing for church the first time I was to wear it, I cried and stamped and said I would never wear it, and poor Della was in despair, not knowing what madame would do if she heard me.

She said: "Look at me, Bessie. My dress is just like yours and I am not saying a word."

I answered: "You never do say a word. If you like it you can wear it, but I'm not going to."

And so it went on until madame's voice was heard, calling on us to start for church; and I let my dear, sweet sister button up my hateful frock and tie on the hateful hat and wipe my eyes and nose with a wet cloth, and we flew down the stairs in time to take our place in the procession; for we always went everywhere in twos, a teacher ahead and one behind. Madame never went to church herself.

My beloved sister must have had an awful time with me. She never did anything wrong or queer, and this year was called not only the most beautiful but the best girl in the school. I was always causing her anxious moments. One night she found me crying bitterly when she came to bed. She asked me anxiously if I were ill.

"Have you earache?"

"No."

"Then what is the matter?"

"Oh, Della, I'm crying because I don't love any one."

"Mercy, Bessie, you don't love me?"

"No. If any one else was as good to me as you are, I'd love them just as much!"

"You certainly are a queer child. You mean to say you don't love mamma?"

"If any one else did all she does for me, I'd care just as much for them."

I sobbed on and poor Della in despair said: "And you don't love papa?"

"Oh, yes, yes," I cried with the greatest relief; "I do love papa."

"Then for mercy's sake stop crying and go to sleep."

CHAPTER XII

SUMMER ON THE SEA—SCHOOL AND DELLA'S
ILLNESS AND TRIP ABROAD—PAPA
ELECTED GOVERNOR

WE went to our summer home on Pawley's Island in June, and oh! the delight of the freedom of the life on the sea-beach after the city, and the happiness of being at home. The bathing in the glorious surf early in the morning — we often saw the sun rise while we were in the water, for we were a very early household, and had breakfast at what would now be thought an unearthly hour, but my father did a tremendous day's work, which could only be accomplished by rising before the sun. And we children were by no means idle. We were required to read and write and practise every day. Papa's rules were strict: we could never go out to walk or play on the beach in the afternoon unless we had done our tasks. I was required to practise only half an hour, but it must be done. Then I wrote a page in a blank book and showed it to mamma for correction. She had me to write a journal of all that had taken place the day before, instead of writing in a copy-book. I have one of the little old books before me now, commonplace and dull, but it was a very good idea for a child, I think. I must have acquired the diary habit then, for all my life it has been a comfort to me to record my joys and my woes, when they were not too deep. Then I read aloud to mamma from some classic for half an hour, so I did not go wild during the holidays. Add to this that papa did not allow us to read a story-book or a novel before the three-o'clock dinner, so that I read by myself in the mornings Motley's "Rise of the Dutch Republic" and Prescott's "Philip II" — only a little portion every day, but there is no telling how much my taste was formed by it.

There were three girls of my own age living on the island, and we met and walked together every afternoon. Jane and Rebecca Alston were twins and exactly alike; there was a tale that their most competent elder sister had once given a dose of medicine to the well one when they were lying in bed together, unable absolutely to tell one from the other. This tale was a comfort to me, for though I was devoted to Rebecca and did not like Jane, when we met I could not possibly tell which was my friend until Jane showed her haughty nature in some way. They called each "Sissy," so there was no help from that. The third girl, Kate La Bruce, was devoted to Jane and disliked Rebecca, but she was as helpless at first as I was. They have all gone to the beyond before me.

Madame had occupied a house in Tradd Street, two doors east of Meeting, that first year; but when we returned in October to school she had moved into a very nice house in Meeting Street, with a delightful big garden full of rose-bushes and violets — such a joy to us, for we could roam about it during recess and in the afternoon. This year another boarder of my own age arrived, Emma Cheves. We looked at each other with suspicious scrutiny for a while, and then we became the most devoted friends. Emma was my first friend and remained my best friend all her life. It was a great grief when she passed away a year ago. She, like myself, lived on a big rice-plantation, so we had much in common, only her beautiful home was very near Savannah.

This winter my dear, sweet, beautiful sister, who never did anything wrong and to whom all the teachers were devoted, was taken ill. It proved to be inflammatory rheumatism, and she was desperately ill. At that day trained nurses were unknown, and it seems a wonder that any one ever got over a desperate illness, but they did. Madame moved Della into her own large, airy room, and she nursed her herself, with the assistance of one of our very good negro servants that papa sent down for that purpose, and who was devoted and vigilant; and after a long illness Della recovered. It was spring when she was able to leave the room. The doctor advised a sea-voyage for her, and papa determined to take mamma and herself abroad. My mother's eldest sister, Mrs. North, offered to take the younger children, with the nurse, Mary O'Shea, while they were gone, to her home, Badwell, Abbeville district, the original home of mamma's people. This was very good of Aunt Jane, as it was quite an undertaking, and for six months.

I do not remember the stay there with any pleasure, though my aunt and cousins were very good to me. I was so miserable about those who had crossed the ocean. I never expected to see them again. The only thing I remember very clearly was dreadful. There was a big boy there who used to tease me and laugh at me. Aunt Jane's coachman, Joe, a very good man, was ill all summer, and I got into the habit of asking to be allowed to take something nice from the dinner-table to him every day, which seemed to please my aunt, and was the thing in the day that gave me most pleasure. One day just before dinner-time this boy called to me: "Come, Bessie, quick. Joe wants to speak to you." I ran breathless, right up the steps, into the room, up to the bed. Joe was just in the agonies of death; a silver dollar hung over each eye — the negro method of closing the eyes in death — his mouth open and teeth all exposed with the last struggle for breath, and the terrible rattle in his throat! No words can describe the effect it had upon me. Day and night he was before my eyes, and the dread sound was in my ears. I became really ill nervously, and they had to pet me and feed me up, and dose me with stimulants.

I don't remember anything more until I was back at home on the plantation with mamma and papa and Della all there, and seeing the lovely things they had brought for us. Then, too, I heard I was not to go to boarding-school again, but was to live with the family in the beautiful house papa had bought and given to mamma in Meeting Street, next to the Scotch church.

Papa brought with him from Paris a beautiful

piano mechanique. It was an upright rosewood piano which could be played naturally like any other, but when you closed the lid on the keys you could open the top, and there was a tiny railroad-track on which you put wooden blocks about one-half inch thick, eight inches long and four wide, and having wires inserted into them much like a wool or cotton card. There was a handle which turned and carried these little flat cars along the track, but it took great skill to turn the handle evenly with the right hand and adjust the little flat cars with the left hand so that they would touch each other and make no break in the music. But dear Nelson, our head house-servant, soon learned to do it beautifully, and it was the greatest delight to him and he was ready to play all the evening. Now that there are so many inventions to give music this does not seem remarkable, but in 1855 it was most wonderful, and the greatest possible joy. We heard all the most beautiful operas and classical music that we never would have heard or known anything about. The music came in little wooden boxes about two feet long and six inches wide and high. They occupied a corner in the drawing-room, and when piled were about four feet high and four feet wide.

The dear little piano was moved during the war to the interior where we refugeed, and it is still in the family — very tired, but still sweet in tone. But the boxes of music were lost during the war. I have often regretted it greatly, because it seems to me it was quite as beautiful as any of the machines I have heard since, and the collection of music was so fine. This piano cost $1,000 in Paris, besides the heavy expense of bringing it over to this country.

My sister took music lessons while in Paris from M. Lestoquoi, a distinguished pianist, and made great strides in her playing; she really was a beautiful musician.

My father was elected governor of the State the next year and as there would be necessarily a great deal of entertaining in which Della would have to take part, papa decided that it would be best for her not to return to school, as it would be impossible for her to keep her mind on her studies. So, though she was only sixteen, she left school. There were balls and receptions and dinners, and though I had no part in them, it was hard for me to study.

All my sister's ball dresses came from Paris, and it was the most exciting thing to see her dress for a ball. At that time they wore the most beautiful artificial flowers, and I especially remember Della in a frock of tulle — little pleatings from waist to floor of white tulle and then pink tulle, and long garlands of apple-blossoms with silver stamen, and a light garland twined in her smooth, glossy brown hair. She was a picture, truly, and naturally she was a great belle and had many suitors. She did not care for attention at all, and I think that only made her the more attractive. She was not allowed to dance the "round dances," as they were called — the waltz, the polka, and the mazurka — as only what was considered the fast set danced them; and a ring of spectators would form round the room to watch the eight or ten girls who were so bold as to dance them.

The proprieties were really worshipped at that time. I remember hearing Della severely scolded for having answered a note from a young man asking her to ride on horseback with him, in the first person. Poor Della said: "But how else could I write, mamma?"

"You should have written: 'Miss Allston regrets that she will not be able to ride with Mr. Blank this afternoon.'"

Such a thing as driving with a young man was

not possible, though at that time all the men had fine horses and buggies. But my sister, being a very good horsewoman, was allowed to ride occasionally with a young man. Girls were not allowed to receive visitors without a chaperon being in the room. Mamma found this part of her duty very trying, so I was sent to study my lessons in the east drawing-room, where my sister received her visitors; and I certainly enjoyed the situation, if no one else did. There was a beautiful drop-light on the table by which I studied at one end of the room. I always murmured my lessons aloud as I swayed backward and forward, to give the impression that I was oblivious to all but my book. But little escaped my ears. As a rule I thought the conversation dull, but one night I heard the young man say, laying his hand on the marble table beside them: "Have you ever seen any one as cold as this marble?"

Della answered composedly: "No."

Then he said: "I am looking now at one whose heart is just as cold." That rather pleased me, but as Della seemed bored he did not proceed in that strain.

Charleston was very gay for a few weeks in the winter at that time. There were three or four balls every week. Three balls given by the St. Cecilia Society took place at intervals of ten days, for everything had to be crowded in before Lent came. These were the most exclusive and elegant balls of all; but the Jockey Club ball, which always ended the race week, was the largest and grandest — not so exclusive, because it included all the racing people. The races were the great excitement of the winter. Every one went and every one bet. Gloves and French sugar-plums came pouring in upon every girl who had any attention at all, for that was the only time that a girl could receive any offering from a man but flowers.

These last were terribly stiff bouquets made up by a florist, with rows of trite roses and pinks and other flowers all wired on to a stick, forming a pyramid with geranium-leaves around the base, surrounded with a white lace-paper frill and wrapped in silver paper. My sister had one suitor who had sense and, instead of sending these terrible stiff pyramids, used to send her little reed baskets filled with little white musk-roses picked by himself in his aunt's garden. They were too sweet — no stems — just a quart of little darlings that you could put in your drawer, and be con-

scious of, every time you took a garment out for
weeks — and so recall the donor. Alas, he was
killed early in the war. This was Pinckney Alston,
a gallant soldier and charming man. My father
was very anxious for Della to learn to sew, and
she was at last spurred to the point of making a
frock for herself. Up to this time her only achieve-
ment in the way of sewing had been when she was
about fourteen and we were at West Point for
brother's graduation. Our great hero, General
Robert E. Lee, then Colonel Lee, was superinten-
dent at that time, and paid Della a great deal of
attention, and one day when he was lamenting
that he had no one to hem six new handkerchiefs,
his wife being absent, mamma suggested to my
sister that she should offer to hem them for him,
which after much hesitation she did. She did not
finish all of them before we left, and sent them
with a little note when we reached home, and
received from him the most charming letter of
thanks, which Della always treasured among her
sacred things. The great success of this venture
with her needle seemed to have completely satisfied her ambition, until papa, to whom she was
perfectly devoted, roused her to attempt and accomplish the great feat of the frock. I well re-

member her appearance when she put it on for the first time. She was very proud of it, and apparently perfectly content with it, but it was a sore trial to me. To begin with, the color displeased me. It was a yellow cambric with little black figures here and there. The skirt was very long and the waist very short and tight; the sleeves were meant to be long but failed of their intention, leaving about three inches of wrist unadorned. No one liked to discourage her first effort by any criticism. She had received from a young man the day before she first donned it, a note requesting an interview alone at twelve o'clock, which had been granted. It did not seem to excite her at all, but I was greatly excited, for this was a very good-looking man, and I had never realized that he was devoted to her, he was so quiet and undemonstrative; but I knew this must mean something, it was so unusual. And I know if he had not been the son of one of papa's best friends, it would not have been permitted. What was my horror, then, when I saw Della going into the drawing-room to this fateful meeting in the yellow cambric frock with its inadequate sleeves! The interview did not last very long, and Della was sufficiently upset, when she rapidly went to her own room, to satisfy even my ideas!

I did not ask any questions, but I gleaned from the family talk that the young man had come to say good-by, as he was to sail for New York on his way to Europe the next day. Just at the hour at which the steamer left a beautiful pyramidal bouquet arrived in a handsome silver bouquet-holder, with Mr. Blank's card.

CHAPTER XIII

CHRISTMAS AT CHICORA WOOD

WHILE we were at boarding-school we had not gone into the country for the short Christmas holidays; but now we went a week before Christmas with all the household, and did not return till about the 10th of January. Oh, the joy of the Christmas on the plantation! We had to have presents for so many — fruit and candy and dolls and nuts and handkerchiefs and stockings and head-handkerchiefs. Rejoicing and festivities everywhere! All busy preparing and selecting Christmas presents, and decorating the house with holly. Christmas Eve, making egg-nog, and going round with little children helping them hang up stockings and, later, going round with grown-ups and filling stockings. Christmas morning very early, "Merry Christmas!" echoing all over the house; all the house-servants stealing in softly to "ketch yu," that is, say the magic words "Merry Christmas!" before you did. Then joyful sounds, "I ketch yu!" and you must produce your gift, whereupon they bring from the ample bosom or pocket, as the case may be, eggs tied in a handkerchief — two, three, six, perhaps a dozen, according to the worldly position of the donor. Such jolly, gay, laughing visitors, a stream coming all the time. As fast as one party left another came, always making great plans to walk softly so as to catch you, so that dressing was a prolonged and difficult matter, for you must respond and open the door when "Merry Christmas, I ketch yu!" sounded. Breakfast was apt to be late, because cook and all the servants had to creep up softly to each door and "ketch" each member and receive their presents, and open them, and exhibit them, and compare them, and see the children's presents, and do an immense deal of unnecessary talking and joking. So that it was hard for them to settle down and come to prayers, which papa had always in the library, and then bring in the breakfast and resume the attitude of respectful and well-trained servants.

Such delicious breakfast — sausage, and hogs-head cheese, and hominy, and buckwheat cakes, and honey and waffles, and marmalade, which mamma made from the oranges which grew all round the piazza. And before we got up from table, the dancing began in the piazza, a fiddle playing the

[151]

gayest jigs, with two heavy sticks knocking to mark the time, and a triangle and bones rattling in the most exciting syncopated time; and all the young negroes on the plantation, and many from the other plantations belonging to papa, dancing, dancing, dancing. Oh, it was gay! They never stopped from the time they began in the morning, except while we were at meals, until ten o'clock at night. The dancers would change, one set go home and get their dinner, while another took the floor. Fiddler, stick-knocker, all would change; but the dance went on with the new set just as gaily as with the first. And this went on more or less for three days, for not a stroke of work was done during that holiday except feeding the cattle, pigs, and sheep, and horses — just three days of pure enjoyment and fun. Christmas night papa always set off beautiful fireworks with Nelson's help. This was a grand entertainment for all, white and black. There was much feasting at Christmas, for a beef and several hogs were always killed and extra rations of sugar, coffee, molasses, and flour were given out, and great quantities of sweet potatoes. Altogether, it was a joyful time.

There were three days at New Year too, and then the clothes were given out. Maum Mary began early in the morning after New Year's Day to bring out and pile in log-cabin fashion in the piazza rolls of red flannel, rolls of white homespun (unbleached muslin), and of thick homespun, and of calico for the women. Then, for the men, rolls of jeans, dark-colored, and rolls of white for shirts, and then rolls of the most beautiful white stuff like the material of which blankets are made. This was called *plains*, and with the jeans was imported from England, as being stronger and warmer than any to be got in this country. There were buttons and threads and needles in each roll of stuff, suitable for that thickness of material. All these little piles made of rolls filled up the very big piazza, and it took nearly all day for the long lists to be read out and each individual to come up and get their stuffs. Each woman had a red flannel roll, two white homespun rolls, two colored homespun, and two calico. The men had one red flannel, two white homespun, two jeans, and one white plains. Then came the blankets. Every year some one got new blankets, very strong, warm wool blankets. One year the men got them, the next the women, the next the children; so every household had some new ones every year.

The children's clothing was given out the next

[153]

day. This took longer. Each child came up to Maum Mary where she sat surrounded by whole bales of stuff, and stood in front of her. She took the end of the homespun, held it on top of the child's head and brought the material down to the floor and then up again to the head. This would make one full garment for the child, and was the way to assure there being enough, with no waste. The red flannel was handled the same way, and the colored homespun for every-day frocks, and the calico for Sunday frocks. It was an interesting thing to watch: a name was read out by mamma, papa, or my sister from the book, and up the step came the little girl, dropped a courtesy to each of us and then to Maum Mary, and stood before her to be measured. Maum Mary was sometimes inclined to be very impatient and cross, but she dared not give way to the inclination openly, with us all watching her. She would just jerk the timid ones around a little; but if papa was there he would say quite sternly: "Gently, Mary, gently." The little girl, as she went out loaded with her things and the things of her little brothers and sisters, would drop another courtesy of thanks. The boys were taught to "Tech dey furud," as Maum Mary called it; being really just what the military salute is now; but they were generally very awkward about it.

The hardest thing of all was the shoes. Every man, woman, and child on the place, about a month before, was called on to give their measure — a nice, light strip of wood about an inch wide the length of their foot. Each was supposed to put the weight of the foot down on the piece of wood and have some one mark and cut it off the right length; then take it himself, so that there would be no mistake, to Mr. Belflowers, who wrote the full name upon it. These measures Mr. Belflowers brought to papa, all clearly and distinctly marked in pencil; and they were sent to the factor in Charleston, who took them to a reliable shoe dealer, and each measure was fitted into a pair of shoes. These shoes were all boxed up and sent up to the different plantations in time for distribution on the third day after New Year. Darkies have a very great dislike of big feet, so many of them were tempted to send too short a measure; and then what a disappointment and what suppressed groans and lamentations when the new shoes were tried on!

"Somebody change my meshur." And often I was called on to examine the stick and read out the name on it. No mistake there. But these victims of vanity were few, and were always much ridiculed by the others who had wisely given the full length of the foot.

"Ki, Breder, yu got small fut, yu kno'. Yu haf' fu suffer. Me, I got big fut an I kin run een my new shu'."

There was much visiting among the neighbors during this season. Every one had friends from the city to spend the holidays in the country. The plantations were large, so the neighbors were not near; but they all had an abundance of horses and vehicles, and the roads were excellent. An absolutely flat country, the dirt roads were kept in the best condition. There were Mr. and Mrs. Poinsett at the White House, eight miles south of Chicora at the point of land between the Pee Dee and the Black Rivers. Mr. Poinsett was a distinguished man, a great botanist. It was he who brought from Mexico the beautiful Flor del Buen Noche to the Department of Agriculture; and it was named Poinsettia in his honor. He was secretary of war under Van Buren and was largely instrumental in the establishment of the Naval Academy at Annapolis. He married Mrs. John Julius Pringle, née Izard, a widow, and made a

most beautiful garden at her plantation, the White
House — so named originally because it was a
little white house in the midst of a field. Mr.
and Mrs. Poinsett spent their summers at Newport and most of the winters in Washington.

Mr. and Mrs. Julius Izard Pringle (née Lynch)
and their daughter Mary, afterward Countess
Yvan des Francs, who was my sister's dearest
friend, being just her age — lived at Greenfield,
eight miles southwest of us on the Black River in
winter, and went to Newport in summer. Mr.
and Mrs. Ralph Izard (née Pinckney) and their
large family lived at Weymouth, six miles south of
us on the Pee Dee. They spent their winters there
and travelled abroad during the summers. Doctor
Sparkman and his family were at Dirliton, five
miles away, Doctor Stark Heriot four miles at
Birdfield, Mr. and Mrs. Nat Barnwell (née Fraser)
at Enfield, three miles away. These were all south
of us.

To the north were Mr. and Mrs. Francis Weston (née Tucker) and their large family. The eldest daughter has been a most remarkable woman.
I speak of her as Miss Penelope in "The Woman
Rice Planter." Mrs. Weston was the daughter of
my father's eldest sister, who married Mr. John

Tucker, had two daughters and died; when Mr. Tucker remarried twice and had a large number of children, — five sons, four of whom he educated in the most thorough manner as physicians, sending them to Paris for a final course, as he said the owner of a plantation with large numbers of slaves could best be fitted for the position by a good medical education. So there were three Doctor Tuckers owning plantations north of us on the Pee Dee River, and one Doctor Tucker owning plantations on the Waccamaw River. They did not practise their profession beyond their plantations, however, but were mighty hunters and good citizens.

Just north of the Weston's historic plantation, Hasty Point, lived at Bel Rive Mr. and Mrs. J. Harleston Read (née Lance). This was entailed property, a part of the very large John Mann Taylor estate. The Reads, like the Westons, spent their summers in Charleston, where they owned beautiful houses. Mrs. Weston, once speaking to my mother of the terrible move to and from the city each spring and fall, said: "We have to take fifty individuals with us in the move, I mean children and all."

My mother: "Why, Elizabeth, how is that possible?"

She answered: "We cannot possibly separate husband and wife for six months; so Harry, the coachman, has to have his wife and children, and the same with the cook, and the butler, and the laundress, until we are actually moving an army every time we move."

This shows some of the bondage of the old system not generally thought of.

CHAPTER XIV

LIFE IN CHARLESTON — PREPARATIONS
FOR WAR

WE returned to Charleston, January the 15th, in the midst of the gay season. Of course, I went back to school and had little to do with the gaiety, except to see Della dress for the balls and hear her account of them the next morning.

I had always suffered much from what I know now was dyspepsia, but it had no name then. I just felt badly at eleven every day if I ate any breakfast. In our family it was considered the proper thing to eat breakfast, and I had always had a fair appetite and ate my plate of hominy and butter, and an egg or a piece of sausage and then a waffle and syrup or honey. That was our regular breakfast; but I began to find, if I ate my plate of hominy, I was perfectly miserable by eleven; and so I ate less and less until I found out the delightful fact that, if I ate nothing, I did not have the misery at eleven. But, when my mother found I was eating no breakfast, she was shocked and distressed and said I could not possibly go to school and study on a perfectly empty stomach. I must eat my hominy — a mother now would say "my cereal." I said: "Just let me eat a waffle and no hominy." But the hominy was considered the most nourishing, easily digested thing, with a soft-boiled egg. As I was always very hungry in the morning, I yielded readily and went on suffering more and more — burning cheeks and flaming eyes and so cross every one was afraid to speak to me from eleven till two. Then it passed off, and I was exhausted and ate a hearty dinner. This went on until I could go no longer. I was too miserable and had to tell mamma and stay in bed. She sent for the family doctor, a white-haired old gentleman, Doctor Peter Porcher. He questioned me and punched me all over with his long forefinger, and then said to me:

"What would you do if you had a horse that was worn out from overwork?"

Very much tried by this question so alien to my condition, I said languidly: "Let him rest, I suppose."

"Exactly," said the little doctor. "Exactly, and that is what we must do to your stomach and digestive organs, which are worn out by overwork."

[161]

Then he asked mamma to have two bedroom pitchers of warm water brought, and he made me drink glass after glass of that tepid water, which he handed me himself, until my system was emptied of every particle of undigested food. Then he said to mamma that for three days I must have absolutely nothing but a cup half full of milk filled up with hot water in the morning, nothing more. He patted my hand and said:

"Then you will be quite well and have no more trouble."

I stayed in bed that day and was so exhausted that I slept and rested and never thought of food; but the next morning, when they brought me my cup of milk and water, I was desperately hungry and very restless. So I sent for mamma and told her that if she kept me in bed I could not possibly endure the three days' fast, for I thought of nothing but how hungry I was; but, if she let me get up and go to school and study my lessons, I would not mind it so much. Mamma hesitated a little, but knew me so well that she was sensible and gave me permission to get up and dress and go to school; which I did, getting there just in time. I said my lessons and enjoyed myself greatly, the freedom from gnawing distress in my chest mak-

ing me very gay; and, at the end of the three days,
I returned to my natural diet and was in perfect
health, and for years free from any kind of indi-
gestion. I just narrate this as an instance of the
heroic methods of the past. We were brought
up to make light of and endure all pain silently
just as long as we could stand it, and then submit
to any treatment prescribed by the doctor, however drastic. For years I had suffered daily pain
and discomfort, but not severe enough to attract
attention to me, as I did not complain, was only
miserable and cross, and correspondingly gay as
soon as the misery was gone. And now I was
well!

In the spring I went to my first child's party.
It was given by the Cleland Hugers in their house
in Legare Street for their beautiful son, two years
older than myself. Alas, he was one of the first
to fall in battle during our war. He and Oliver
Middleton were both so beautiful and both fell
gallantly fighting when mere boys. But there
was no shadow in that bright scene to tell us
what was coming. Mamma had a pretty white
muslin frock made for me, and my sweet sister
took great pleasure in dressing me for the party
— a very full, very short skirt barely covering

my knees, a long expanse of white stocking, and black slippers. When I stood before the big cheval glass, Della fixing some blue ribbons on my tightly scraped back, tightly plaited hair, I began to cry and exclaimed:

"Della, I am too ugly to live! I can't go to the party!"

My dear sister expostulated and assured me I looked sweet, and said how pretty my frock was, etc., etc., but it only added fuel to fire; and I cried the more. At last she lost patience and said:

"Well, if you go on crying, you *will* be a sight with red, swollen eyes and nose" — and I stopped at once, and let her bathe them, and try to remove some of the damage; and I went down.

It was an awful ordeal, for Charley was invited, too, and May, the Irish nurse, was sent to take us; and, when she got to the door, she asked to see Mrs. Huger and commended us specially to her care. Charley had never been to a party before. He looked beautiful in his Scotch plaid kilt mamma had brought from abroad; but he was very frightened and, just as soon as Mrs. Huger released his hand, he found a safe place behind a door where he could see and not be seen, nor be in

danger of receiving any attention. Mrs. Huger
took me into the dancing-room, and immediately a
small boy I knew, who had long golden curls, asked
me to go to supper with him. I gladly accepted, for
I had had visions of no partner for supper, which
was the greatest catastrophe which could happen.
So I was quite pleased to accept my very youthful
beau; but in a few minutes more the biggest boy
in the room came and asked me for supper! And
I had to say I was engaged! It was dreadful. I
hated my golden curled devoted, with a fierce
hatred. And it was worse when supper came, for
I suddenly remembered my responsibility about
Charley, who had to be provided with supper;
and my little partner seemed reluctant to help me
look for him. The rooms were crowded and it
was dreadful to roam around alone looking for
Charley, and when at last I found him behind the
door he was crying; but, after I took his hand and
led him to the supper-room with its beautiful
cakes with a cupid on a wire on top of each, and
the dishes of ice-cream and cakes, and silver dishes
of candy and kisses, he soon recovered. And I
found that my little beau had busied himself,
while I was gone, getting three saucers of ice-
cream and three slices of cake, so he rose in my

estimation; and the party ended most happily. And I found, though I was ugly, boys liked to talk to me and to dance with me, which, after all, was the main thing.

These years were very happy ones. Mamma enjoyed the return to the social life of the city very much after her long experience of country life; and, of course, it was a joy to have her lovely daughter to introduce into society. My sister was absolutely docile and did just what mamma wanted her to do. She never had a wish about her own clothes, and no wonder, for mamma had perfect taste and got everything for her that was beautiful.

About this time I remember two little experiences of my own. My dear sister had always been willing to share her high-post mahogany bed and beautiful room with me; but papa thought I should have my own room, as I was old enough. So the room next to hers was fitted up for me and was just as pretty as could be, with its own tall four-poster and pretty chintz curtains and with the bathroom attached. But still I slept in Della's room, though I dressed and kept my clothes in my own room. But one day when papa returned from Columbia he asked me if I slept well in my own beautiful bed now; and the truth had to come out that I never had slept there, at which he looked grave and said: "It is my wish that you sleep in your own room." So that night I did so, and the following night also, and began to think I should end by liking it. It was spring and all the windows were open, and the third night I was awakened by shrieks from Price's Alley, which ran along beside our garden wall! Screams and cries for help and sounds of blows falling! It was just as distinct as if it had been in the next room. I fled to Della's room and never again attempted to sleep in my own room. The next morning we heard it was a drunken man beating his wife; some Irish families occupied a house together there. But it was the end of papa's efforts to make me a self-respecting individual. I stayed with my sister until she was married, and then I took my younger sister, whom I adored, in with me. She was five years younger than myself, but a very different nature, as brave as a lion. Nothing scared her nor made her nervous.

The other experience was, I know, some years later, for I was big enough to have boy, as well as girl friends; and one afternoon mamma told me I could have the open carriage to take some of my friends for a drive. I was much delighted and invited Minnie Hayne and Willie Wilkinson, and Minnie invited another boy. We were having a very nice time, and Minnie was in such a gale of spirits that she began to sing, and the boys joined in, and I began to feel a little nervous for fear we might meet some of my family, when the carriage stopped and Daddy Aleck, the coachman, who always sat as straight as if he had been trained at West Point, turned stiffly round and said:

"Miss Betsy, if unna (you-all) kyant behave unna self, I'll tek yu straight home! Dis ain't no conduk fu de Gubner karridge!"

My feelings are better imagined than described. However, it was most successful. The rest of the drive was perfectly proper; and after a while when we got up the road one of the boys brought out a box of sugar-plums, which we ate most noiselessly and discreetly, and we had a delightful drive and mamma never heard of our undue hilarity. These seem very trivial things to record, but young girls are interested in trivial things; and the surge of events toward the great Civil War, which was approaching, was not felt by me at all. I realized more and more the beauty and comfort of my home and surroundings.

I must describe our servants. Nelson was the butler and house-servant. (He was a mulatto, the son of a Mr. Thompson who had been overseer at Chicora before Mr. Belflowers. He was a Northern man, very smart and capable; but after this papa sent him away. Nelson adopted his father's surname, Thompson.) He was the best, most faithful, intelligent man possible, and we were all devoted to him. Then came William Baron, who was very black and very heavily built, but an excellent servant, with very courteous manners. He took the greatest delight in arranging all the flowers in the house, which I also loved to do; and there was always a race between William and myself as to who should do it. I remember specially one yellow flat bowl on a stand with Greek figures in black chasing round it, a perfectly lovely thing for flowers; and it nearly broke my heart when I found William had changed the flowers in it and arranged them to his mind. William was my brother's (Colonel Ben Allston's) body-servant during the whole war.

After the war William Baron became well known in Charleston as a caterer, cook, and provider of elegant entertainments. He took charge of the suppers for the St. Cecilia, which were always very handsome and elaborate and quite a feature. Indeed, William was quite a personage, with grand manners, and perfectly honest. He had but one fault, to look upon the wine when it was red; he habitually took more than was good for him and lived too high, so that his health gave out before he was at all an old man. He always showed enthusiastic pleasure when he met any of the family, but especially my eldest brother to whom he had belonged. Mas' Ben continued to fill his ideas as to what constituted a gentleman. Whenever my brother came to the city and he knew it, he would send round a dish of delicious chicken salad or a shrimp pie, for which he was famous, or a Charlotte Russe, or some dish that he knew Mas' Ben specially liked. It was always a pleasure to meet William; his very black, round face shone with delight and every one of his very white teeth showed, as he assured you that "it did his heart good to look upon you and you were looking so fine and so well."

Then there was Stephen Gallant, who was papa's special servant and valet, but when there was much company he helped with the waiting, which he understood well. Joe Washington was the cook. He had been trained two years by a

man who kept a very fine restaurant, Sam Lee.
Phœbe and Nannie were the maids, and Nellie,
Nelson's wife, the laundress, assisted by a young
girl. Daddy Moses, William's father, was brought
down from the country to take charge of the yard
and be gardener under a white man, Mr. Wubb,
who was employed. Harris, a boy in the house,
attended the bell and ran errands. They were all
good servants and I was fond of all but Stephen,
whom I could not bear. He put on great airs because he went with papa to Columbia always, and
felt himself superior to the others, who jokingly
called him the "little guv'ner," because he imi-
tated papa's walk and manner generally, in an
absurd way, as he was quite small and very black.

My sister became engaged the year before the
war. She had a beautiful engagement ring, a
diamond. She also wore always a magnificent
ruby which had been left her by Uncle Tom, captain in the navy. One day she was sewing before
dinner and had taken off her rings and slipped
them into her work-box, and when we went in to
dinner she left it in the hall. When we came out
from dinner and she opened her work-box to get
the rings, they were gone! It is a very remarkable thing that the servants were not suspected at

all. There was a door in the hall opening on to
the driveway, and it was always taken for granted
that a thief had slipped in, opened the box, and
taken out the only valuables in it and escaped.
The police were notified to look out for a sneak-
thief, and they reported great activity on their
part, ending in nothing. The rings were never
heard of again. My sister was much blamed for
her carelessness. I know now that poor Stephen
took those rings. He was not waiting on table
that day, and knew well the value of the jewels
and my sister's habit of slipping them off into her
box while she was sewing. He knew about the
approaching war, and he knew they would always
command a good sum of money, for the great
value of the pigeon-blood ruby had often been
discussed. And Stephen was the only one who
ran off to the U. S. fleet before the end of the con-
flict. Soon after my father's death he took his
whole family but one boy, Brutus, put them in a
small boat and rowed through the waves from the
inlet next to Pawley's Island and joined the fleet.
It must have all been arranged before, for they
were on the lookout for the boat and picked them
up safely. Of course, this was a great risk, and
it seems strange, after braving the waves of the
ocean in a small boat, Stephen should have been

drowned some years after the war in the Wacca-maw River. He had overloaded his boat with rough rice and it sank. His son Brutus, who was with him, escaped by swimming to shore.

When the family went into the country this year, early in December, my aunt Ann (Uncle Tom's widow, the buying of whose negroes at her urgent request ruined my father) asked mamma to leave me with her, so that I could continue at school until the holidays and so not lose my place in my classes. So I stayed and went to school from her house. The holidays began December 20. I was to take the steamer *Nina*, which was the only way to reach Georgetown then except to travel the sixty miles in our own carriage, as my mother always did; but, of course, mamma and the family having gone that way, I had to take the boat. It so happened that the day for the sailing of the *Nina* was a day of wild excitement, as it was the 20th of December, 1860. The Ordinance of Secession was passed that morning in Charleston, and the whole town was in an uproar. Parades, shouting, firecrackers, bells ringing, cannon on the forts booming, flags waving, and excited people thronging the streets. I was to go on board the *Nina* at nine o'clock and sleep there, as she sailed at an unearthly hour in the morning.

[173]

My aunt's coachman was to drive me down, but he came to her and said:

"Miss, I cudn't possible keep dem horse frum run, wid all dis racket. Dem is jest de trimble en prance een de stable now, en I dasn't dare tek dem on de street."

We all knew they were very spirited, overfed horses, and that the man was right. It would be a great risk to attempt to drive them. So it was decided I would have to walk. My two cousins had come to see me off and walked with me — J. Johnston Pettigrew, my great hero and ideal of a man; and Charley Porcher, who was only a little older than myself and my great friend. Fortunately my trunk had been sent down in the morning. It had rained and when we got down to the wharf it was wet and muddy, and I had no overshoes. Without a word of warning, Cousin Johnston picked me up in his arms and carried me all the way to the boat. I was overcome by the struggle within me, mortification that I should be treated like a child when I was fifteen and thought myself grown up, and delight and gratification that Cousin Johnston cared enough for me to do it, and joy that I was in the arms of my adored hero! I never saw Cousin Johnston again. He entered the army at once and, after distinguishing himself in every action and being promoted to be general, he was killed at Gettysburg, a terrible loss to our army, and my first sorrow.

South Carolina having seceded from the Union, military preparations began at once. My brother Ben, who had been educated at West Point and served in the army until three years before, raised and equipped a company of cavalry at his own expense, aided by my father. It was called "Marion's Men of Winyah." The whole country was in wild excitement, drilling and preparing for war. Every one volunteered, old, young, and middle-aged. It was hard to keep the boys at school. In the spring every man we knew in Charleston was in one company or another. The Charleston Light Dragoons and the Washington Light Infantry were the favorites, but there were many other companies of great popularity.

One State after another followed South Carolina's example, and a convention was called at Montgomery, Ala., which elected Jefferson Davis President of the Southern Confederacy.

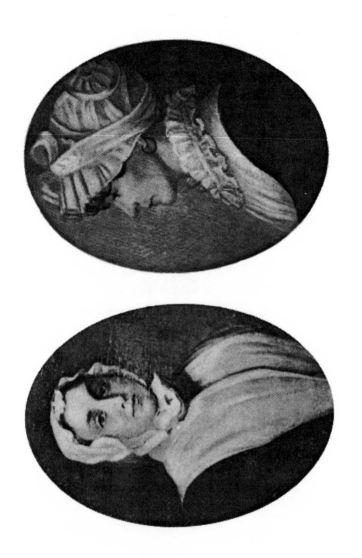

MRS. WILLIAM ALLSTON (left) and MRS. BENJAMIN ALL-
STON (right), Grandmother and Mother, respectively, of
Governor R. F. W. Allston

MR. AND MRS. ROBERT FRANCIS WITHERS ALLSTON.
Portraits by Flagg, *circa* 1850.

CHAPTER XV

BOARDING-SCHOOL IN WAR TIMES

AS soon as war was declared Madame Togno moved her school from Charleston to Columbia, as every one knew it was only a question of time as to when the city would be shelled. She rented Barhamville, a well-known old school a few miles out of Columbia, and in November, 1862, my little sister and myself were sent there. The journey is specially impressed on me, for my eldest sister had talked a great deal of Mary Pringle's delightful brother, Julius, who had left Heidelberg (where he had graduated and was then taking a law course) as soon as he heard of secession, and had run the blockade to join the Confederate army. She had been at home when he called and I had not, and she talked so much about him that I said, with my sharp tongue: "That seemed a strange way for a girl engaged to one man to talk of another, and wondered how her fiancé would like it if he could hear." She did not in the least mind this, but continued her praise, so that my opposition was roused; and, when, as we were taking the train, with packages and much impedimenta, our good Phibby included, for she was to go with us, Della brought up the young man and introduced him to us, I said to her when he went to make some inquiry at the office for her: "So this is your paragon! You certainly shouldn't choose for me!" However, he was a most attentive companion on the journey, and stood and talked to me all the way to Charleston, where we were to spend a few days before going on to Columbia. Jinty made me very miserable, because I was painfully dignified and speaking in the most correct and careful way, till I saw that while he stood and talked to me, she, on the opposite seat, was shooting peanuts skilfully into his coat-pockets. I could not speak to her and reprimand her, for she would have answered me back promptly, and I was terribly afraid he would turn and see what my little sister was doing. He did not, however, and must have been much amazed later to find his pockets full of peanuts.

Barhamville was much larger than any house madame had ever rented before, and so she had many more boarders, and the character of the school was somewhat altered. She still tried to make French the language of the school, but it

[177]

was much harder to carry this out. Most of the girls were eighteen or nineteen and knew no French, so that it was impossible for them to converse in it. Finding this the case, madame made a rule that no one should speak at table except to say, "Passez moi le pain s'il vous plait," and all the other necessary requests for food; for we had two long tables and only one waitress. Madame walked up and down the room while we ate, so as to keep order. Very soon she began to find it very hard to get the good food on which she always prided herself. Tea and coffee had to be left out, and one thing after another, until we ceased to come into the dining-room at all for supper. Two large trays of very dry corn-dodgers were brought into the schoolroom at tea-time, accompanied by two large pitchers of water and a tray of glasses. The girls were all very good and never complained. Every one knew there were privations in their own homes, and felt that madame was doing the best she could for us.

Madame had been fortunate enough to secure very good teachers. Mademoiselle le Prince, the French teacher, was quite a remarkable woman as far as teaching went. Educated at a convent just outside of Paris, she had the best accent, and it was her one idea in life to give a correct and thorough knowledge of French; not only to have her pupils speak it correctly, but to have them write with perfect precision all the difficult terminations of the "participe passé." She was hated by many girls, she was so cross, but she was a delight to me, for she was the real thing. I spoke French glibly and wrote it in the same easy way, to my own satisfaction, but when I got mademoiselle's point of view I was heartily ashamed of my French and very soon rectified all that by hard study, to her delight. The teacher of English was the Reverend Mr. Johnson. He helped out his salary, which was inadequate to his needs, by mending shoes, which he did well.

The music teacher, Monsieur Torriani, was also a joy. Thoroughly competent, most appreciative of good work, it was a delight to work for him. My music had become my great pleasure; and, when I took my first lesson from this charming, appreciative Italian, I felt I was going to have a delightful year at school, whatever the privations might be. Madame assigned me two hours for practice, but very soon I felt that was not enough and begged her to let me have another hour. She said it was impossible; there were only three pianos in the school and I already had more than my share of these three. I still worried her, and at last she said: "If you are willing to get up early and practise an hour on the piano in the drawing-room, you may do it; but it will be hard, for it will have to be before the fire is made up." I accepted with many thanks; and all that winter I got up at six, broke the ice in my pitcher to perform my hasty ablutions, and putting on my cloak took my candle into the drawing-room, and often with tears rolling down my cheeks practised that hour! My hands were so swollen with chilblains that I was ashamed to take my music lesson.

I began to take singing lessons, too, and spent the whole of six months on exercises before I took a single song. I can never forget my delight when Monsieur Torriani applauded my first song — a very high, lovely little song from the opera of "Martha." "Dormi pur ma, il mio riposo tu m'ai tolto, ingrato cor Buona notte, buon dormir." I had a very small, sweet voice, with clear, birdlike, high notes, but it seemed so very little, for we had a girl in school with a beautiful big voice, Sallie McCoullough, such a sweet, good, simple girl. If she had been more sophisticated she would have had a happier life. M. Torriani took delight in training and developing her voice, which was quite fit for opera, but she was no actress, and failed to make the success she should have made through that. Dear, big, sweet, simple Sallie! Every one loved her, and when we got her to sing "Home, Sweet Home" and other old songs in the schoolroom in the dusk without accompaniment, we all wept quarts. One day I said to M. Torriani that I was going to stop my singing lessons, that I had no voice and it was only a mortification.

He asked with a great air of respect: "Did you think of going on the stage?"

"Oh, Monsieur Torriani, don't make fun of me. I am too wretched. I have so little voice, it really is none, and I would so love to sing."

Then he sobered down and said: "Mademoiselle, you must not stop. Your voice is little but very sweet and vous avez le feu sacré. You cannot stop. You will give more pleasure all your life than many a big voice. You will bring comfort to the sad heart. No, you must not stop, you!"

Then he went on to ask how long I practised at a time, and I told him half an hour. "Oh, nevair,

nevair," he exclaimed, and told me never to practise more than ten minutes at one time, and to
spare and protect my "precious little instrument,"
as he called it, in every way. Never to talk loud
or shout, never under any circumstances to talk
in a carriage or car while it was in motion, and
many other directions.

Clothes were becoming difficult. You could
buy nothing, and it was much colder up here than
with us on the coast. We needed cloaks, both
Jane and I. So mamma had Maum 'Venia make
for us each a coat from the lovely white *plains*,
which was bought for the negroes, with pearl buttons taken from some old coats. They were immensely admired and were so nice and warm. It
was just like having a coat made out of the white
part of a very fine, soft blanket, and not the least
part of the joy of them was that they were very
becoming.

It was this winter that my second great friend
came into my life, Ruth Nesbitt, from Georgia.
She was the loveliest, sweetest girl, a tall, very
slender brunette with beautiful brown eyes, and a
little tiptilted nose and a large but well-formed
mouth full of exquisite little teeth. She was so
quiet, so shy, so reserved and stiff. For a long

time I could only tell by her eyes that Ruth cared for me. I was greatly surprised when I found myself devoted to her. I cared for so few and was so easily bored. I constantly had girls devoted to me whose advances I barely endured, and now to find a perfectly congenial companion was too delightful. And to see the color rush over her pretty pansy-looking face, and her bright brown eyes sparkle as I came near was a joy. Travelling was so expensive that we did not go home for the Christmas holidays, and Ruth and I read Dickens out under the trees every day. One sewed while the other read aloud, and it was perfect bliss.

The news from the war became more and more exciting. I had letters nearly every week from my cousin, Hal Lesesne, who was captain in the army and stationed at Battery Wagner. They made me feel I was in the midst of the fighting, they were so vivid, although very short. One day one came, quite a long letter this time, but only a few words legible, the rest soaked with ink. On a scrap of paper he wrote: " Just as I finished this a shell burst near me and a fragment shattered the ink-stand. I send it because I do not know when I can write again and you may be able to make out some of it. Anyway, you will know that I have written." I kept all these letters. They were such a picture of the life there; and, by a strange fate, they were stolen in 1870. It was a great regret to me, for he was killed almost with the last shot which was fired during the war. I was very fond of him. He was not a lover, only a dear friend and cousin; and, besides that feeling, the letters were history by that time, telling of the heroic defense of Batteries Wagner and Gregg and the other fortifications on Morris Island.

PART IV

WAR TIMES

CHAPTER XVI

THE WEDDING

I LEFT school on my birthday, May 29, 1863, and returned to my home in Charleston. There great activity and excitement reigned, for my sister was to be married June 24 and I was to be first bridesmaid. The wedding was very beautiful. To begin with, Della was lovely beyond words, an ideal picture of a bride, and the groom, Arnoldus Van der Horst, was a handsome and martial figure in his uniform, that of a major of the Confederate army. They were married by the assistant rector of St. Michael's Church, the Reverend Mr. Elliot, in our beautiful oval drawing-room or ballroom. It had a very high ceiling and was papered in white with small sprigs of golden flowers scattered over it. There were four large windows on the south, opening on the iron balcony which ran round on the outside. And, on the opposite side of the room, two windows exactly like those opening on the balcony, running from the tall ceiling to the floor, but the panes of these were mirrors. It made you think you were looking into another crowded room. There was a high mantelpiece of white wood carved with exquisite figures of women dancing and holding aloft garlands of flowers, Adam's most beautiful designs; the cornice around the ceiling was also beautiful; the furniture was rosewood, covered with blue velvet with little pink rosebuds, and the carpet was velvet with bouquets of pink roses tied with blue ribbons. The first groomsman, Lewis Van der Horst, brother of the groom, was also in uniform, that of a private in the Charleston Light Dragoons, C. S. A. He was killed the following spring in Virginia, fighting gallantly.

I have a foolish little journal I wrote at this time, so foolish and lacking in all interest, that I do not use it, but think perhaps this little excerpt may be pardoned:

"Charleston, June 27th, 1863.

"Della is married! !

"It all seems like a dream; all the excitement is over, and now for the first time I can think over it calmly. Wednesday at nine the wedding took place. It was a very beautiful ceremony. She was perfectly lovely. Her costume was a full plain dress of Brussel's net, a beautiful material, over a splendid white silk, with a beautiful real lace veil falling almost to the ground; a wreathe of white hyacinths and bouquet of the same.

Such was her costume, but her appearance I cannot describe!"

This diary is a help as to dates, and it records that on July 10, at daybreak, the shelling of Charleston began, and records also the hasty packing up of the household gods and family impedimenta, and their removal from the city; also our arrival at the station at Society Hill, Darlington County, that night at twelve. There had been no time to send orders for Daddy Aleck and the carriage to meet us, but the wonderfully kind neighbors whom we were to find there gave their evidences of generous friendship that night; for John Williams happened to be there and offered his carriage and so did Doctor Smith, so that we got to Crowley Hill with little delay. This was to be our place of refuge during the war, while the plantations on the coast were regarded as unsafe.

Before we left the city there comes to my mind a very vivid picture of a visit paid by another member of the Charleston Light Dragoons, also a private. He was at home on a short furlough and called to pay his respects to my mother, and she sent for me to see him also. It was in the same beautiful oval drawing-room. Mamma was seated on the little sofa in front of one of the mirror windows, and when I entered the room, on a chair facing her and talking with great animation sat Poinsett Pringle, whom I had never seen before, the almost twin brother of my future husband. Introductions were made, and I sat down and listened and looked, and looked and listened. Efforts were made both by himself and by mamma to draw me into the conversation, but in vain. When he had gone mamma said to me:

"Well, Bessie, if this is the way you are going to behave, you certainly will not be a success in society! You sat there with your mouth wide open, gazing at the young man! What was the matter?"

I said solemnly: "Mamma, he was so beautiful that I was paralyzed! I never saw any one so beautiful in my life."

And it was true. He was angelically beautiful; light-brown hair parted in the middle, with a curl in it, short as it was; wonderful blue eyes that looked like windows to a beautiful soul, fair, smooth skin, perfect teeth, and a dimple in his smooth chin — add to this very beautiful hands and the sweetest voice, and no one will wonder that my breath had been taken away by the sight of him. He was the darling and pride of his whole family. His mother had him educated for the diplomatic service. He was a most accomplished musician, playing beautifully on the piano, and had a charming voice. I never saw him again. All this charm and beauty of mind and body was snuffed out by a bullet the following May. I think it was the battle of Haws Shop in Virginia, which the Confederates lost, and had to give up the field. Poinsett was going out unhurt when he saw his friend Bee lying wounded. Poinsett picked him up and carried him some distance toward the rear, when a bullet struck, killing them both. If I could paint, how I would love to perpetuate that beautiful face and figure.

It was a terrible undertaking to pack all that big, heavy furniture and get it away under stress. We found afterward that we had left many things of great value. At this moment I remember especially two blue china Chinese vases, urn-shaped, which stood two feet high and were very heavy. It seemed impossible to get boxes and material to pack them and they were left. Daddy Moses remained alone to take charge of the house and garden.

CHAPTER XVII

CROWLEY HILL — OUR PLACE OF REFUGE DURING THE WAR

CROWLEY HILL, the place to which we went, was a quaint old-fashioned house set in a great grove of oak-trees, not the big live oaks we were accustomed to, but Spanish oaks and red oaks and scrub oaks, which are beautiful in summer and brilliant-colored in autumn, but bare all winter. There was quite a little farm land attached, and the place had been lent papa by the widow of his dear friend, Nicholas Williams. Nicholas Williams, like my uncle, James L. Petigru, was opposed to secession, and when he found himself powerless to influence his State, he determined to leave it and live abroad — but it killed him. He died in New York before sailing. It is impossible to tell the kindness we received from these friends all the time we were refugees in their midst. Of course we were much cut off from our supplies; until mamma had a garden planted and our dairy was got going we were stranded; but every day came servants bringing supplies of every kind, milk, cream, vegetables, fruit, flowers, everything we did not have. At last I said one day to mamma:

"I cannot stand this. I hate to receive! I am accustomed to give, and so are you! I don't see how you stand it, saying 'Thank you' all the time."

Mamma laughed and said: "My child, you are not worthy to give if you cannot receive gracefully. It shows that you think too much of your power to give, and it makes you feel superior! I love to give and am thankful for the many years I have been able to help my neighbors and others in that way; and now I receive with pleasure these evidences of the affection and interest of my dear generous friends."

But never did I get over the feeling of impatience at the necessity of receiving those daily trays and baskets of delicious things. Our household consisted only of mamma, my little sister, and myself, for papa remained at his work on the plantation, only coming now and then for a few days; and Charley having left the country school, Mr. Porcher's, to which he had gone at nine, and where he had endured much hardship from the scarcity of food the year we were at Barhamville, having lived for months on nothing but squash and hominy, had now gone to the Arsenal, the military school in Columbia. We had the full force of servants, except that William was in the army with my brother, who was serving as colonel of the 4th Alabama Regiment in Virginia, and Stephen, who was on the plantation with papa. Mamma at once began to plant the farm and garden, with the house-servants, and made wonderful crops.

I went for a month to visit my sister in Wilmington, Major Van der Horst being on General Whiting's staff, stationed at Wilmington. Mr. McCrea had lent them his beautiful and convenient house, so that my sister was delightfully situated there, and the society was very gay. The first party I went to I made a great mistake. A very handsome man, young De Rosset, asked me to dance as soon as he was introduced. I accepted with pleasure, as I was devoted to dancing. As we stood preparatory to the start, he asked: "Do you dance fast or loose?" I was confused and stammered out, "Oh, I made a mistake. I do not dance at all!" and sat down. I could not bear to say "fast" nor could I bear to say "loose"; but, as I looked at the dancers, I understood what it meant, and there was nothing to terrify me in it. One-half of the dancers held hands crossed, as you do in skating. This was "loose," and the rest danced in the ordinary way which I had always been accustomed to; this was called "fast." This marred my pleasure in the many parties I went to while in Wilmington; for, once having said I didn't dance, I had to stick to it.

The price of every article of clothing was enormous, and shoes were impossible. I thought of buying a pair of stays, but a very common pair were fifty dollars, so I ripped up some old Paris ones and made a beautiful pair for myself, using all the bones, etc. Mamma wrote me to get three yards of material to make a coat to wear next winter. It was ninety-five dollars a yard, the only stuff I could get, thick and hairy, but not fine at all.

At Society Hill, when I returned, the loom was set up in the wash-kitchen, and I learned to weave as well as to spin, and we knit, knit, knit all the time. We had one of the maids to spin a fine yarn of cotton and silk ravellings, with which we knit gloves for our own use. All pieces of old black silk were cut into small scraps and ravelled out and carefully mixed with the cotton, and made a very pretty gray for gloves. We had only one caddy of tea, which was kept for sickness, and a very little coffee. As a substitute, people used bits of dried sweet potato parched, and Indian corn parched, also the seed of the okra; this made a very rich drink, very full of oil. The root of the sassafras made a very nice tea. Sugar was very scarce, so mamma planted sorghum, a kind of sugar-cane which made very nice molasses, which Nelson boiled in the big copper kettle. I made delicious preserves with honey, and we dried figs, and mamma made all the vinegar we used with the fig-skins, put in a cask and fermented. This winter there was trouble about the supplies for the negroes. There were no blankets to be had, and papa wrote, begging mamma to have the carpets cut up into blanket sizes, so that those who were expecting blankets that year should not be disappointed. The thick damask curtains were cut up for coats, as they made good coats, thickly lined. Altogether there was so much to do that the days were not long enough.

One day we had a visit from Julius Pringle, who was on furlough at the house of an uncle, who was refugeeing about four miles away. This was only the second time I saw him. Mamma and he did all the talking, while I sewed in silence. Mamma went out of the room to order some cake and wine, and he told me he didn't know the way to Crowley, and had come to a place where four roads crossed, and was puzzling how to decide which road to take "when I saw a track of a tiny foot leading this way, and I followed that and I knew it would bring me to you." This made me very angry indeed, and I got red and lost the use of my quick tongue. When mamma came back the talk flowed on as easily and pleasantly as possible. She told him what a fine crop of rye she had made in her calf pasture, and what difficulty she had to find a place to put it until she thought of the big piano box, which had helped very much, for it held so much. All this time I sewed in silence, with flaming face. At last he asked me to play. I declined fiercely, but mamma said: "My dear Bessie! Of course you will play for us" — she being quite shocked at my manner. I went to the piano and played as though I were fighting the Yankees. When I returned to my seat Mr. Pringle thanked me, and, turning to my mother, said:

"Mrs. Allston, apparently the piano box is of

more use than the piano!" And then they both laughed heartily.

I could have killed him without hesitation. I saw him at church after that, only a moment. And then the day he was to leave to go back to Virginia, mamma wanted to ask him to take a letter, and we drove to the station. And when he shook hands with me and said good-by, the look in his eye was a revelation and declaration of devotion that seemed to compass me and seal me as forever his, near or far, with my own will or without it. From that moment I knew that no other man could be anything to me. It was so strange that in absolute silence, with not a second's prolonging of the hand-pressure necessary to say a proper, conventional good-by, my whole life was altered; for up to that moment I had no idea that he was devoted to me.

I had always longed to take part in the work going on everywhere for our soldiers. In our little isolated corner we could do nothing but sewing and knitting. Soldiers' shirts made by an extraordinarily easy pattern which some one had invented we made in quantities. All the ladies in Columbia were cooking and meeting the soldier trains day and night, and feeding them and asking what they needed and supplying their wants. They took it by turns, so that no hour of the day or night could a train come and find no one to give them hot coffee and biscuits and sandwiches, and sometimes fried chicken, too.

CHAPTER XVIII

SORROW

WHEN the spring came papa made us a little longer visit than usual. He was not feeling well, his heart was giving him trouble. I only knew this afterward from mamma, for papa never complained. I remember from my early childhood looking on in wonder at the self-denial he exercised, not once or twice, but all the time. His digestion was weak, and day after day, when we had such delicious things, shrimp, fish, and rice-birds, and coots, and green corn, and lima beans, I saw him dine on a plate of milk-and-rice, or a plate of soup with all the delicious okra and tomatoes and beans strained out. But he never talked of it, nor did it make him cross. He was specially tender and gentle to us all this time. One day he asked me to do something and I answered:

"Papa, I don't know how, I can't do it."

And he laid his hand on my shoulder and said: "Don't ever say that, my daughter. God has given it to you that whenever you put your whole self to accomplish anything you will succeed.

When you fail it will be because you have not tried hard enough. Don't forget this; it is a great responsibility. Never say again you cannot do a thing!" He spoke so solemnly that I was greatly impressed; and, many times in my life when things have risen up before me which have seemed quite beyond my strength and capacity and endurance, I have remembered that conversation and gone ahead, only to find that he was right.

When papa said he must go back to the plantation, mamma thought it a great risk, as he was so far from strong. She urged him to take another week's rest; but he said he must go; there was to be a meeting in Georgetown to determine something about the public schools, and he must be there. He would take two days on the drive through the country home, and rest two days before the meeting, for it was most important. He left us March 18, Friday, promising to return to us the next Sunday week.

About a week after he left, early in the morning, a messenger came up on horseback with a note from Mr. Belflowers. He thought it his duty to let mamma know that he thought papa an ill man. He had attended a meeting in Georgetown in very inclement weather, when he was so far from well that he had a mattress put in the carryall, and lay on that instead of going in the carriage. He was afraid "the governor," as he continued to call papa, would not like it if he knew he was writing this, but he had to do it. Mamma ordered the carriage at once and we prepared to start on the journey. By the mail which came in just before we started, a letter came from papa to her, saying he had taken a bad cold and wished very much he could come back and put himself under her care. That was so much for him to admit that she felt she could name the letter as the cause of her coming and not betray Mr. Belflowers. It was dreadful to have no quicker means of going. We started at nine o'clock; that night we spent at Mrs. Fryer's, about half-way. The next morning we started by dawn, met a fresh pair of horses, Mr. Belflowers sent to meet us at Union Church, and reached Chicora about five in the afternoon.

When we got to Chicora we found papa very ill. He had pneumonia. He was very happy to see us and did not inquire why we came. It seemed quite natural to him that we did come. Doctor Sparkman, the same who had saved his life at The Meadows when they were both young, was in attendance and was perfectly devoted.

Stephen was in constant attendance and very efficient, also a very faithful man named John Locust,
sent by my cousin, William Allan Allston, over
from Waccamaw. As soon as I came I was established in the position of head nurse, for I had always had a turn for nursing and at school had
nursed all the sick girls and got the nickname of
Miss Nightingale. I was truly thankful for my
experience now, for I was able to be a comfort to
papa and a help to everybody, specially mamma,
who was completely unnerved by seeing papa so
desperately ill. The doctor had told us he had
little hope, but I was full of confidence that he
would get well. I was very happy to find papa's
comfort in my nursing. I could see his eyes follow me as I moved about the room, and one day
as I brought him his cup of gruel he said, "Daughter, that is a pretty dress; it pleases me" — and
he held the fold of the skirt in his fingers as he
reluctantly swallowed the gruel which I gave him
by the teaspoonful. His breathing was so labored
it was hard for him to speak and also to swallow.
No one can understand the joy his words gave
me, for I loved him so dearly and it was such a
delight to give him pleasure now. I remember
the frock well. It was a greenish-gray material,

something like mohair, with dark-green conventionalized leaves here and there over it; an old dress Della had given me when she got new things for her trousseau. I had had it washed and made it over myself. I kept it just to look at for years and years.

The neighbors helped. Mr. Josh La Bruce came over from Sandy Island in his boat and sat up one night, and was a great help, he was so quiet and so strong in lifting. Then one night Mr. Weston came and sat up and Mr. Belflowers sat up one night. Then Mr. La Bruce came again. Papa suffered terribly from the difficulty of breathing and the want of sleep was dreadful. He could not sleep. He would repeat in a low voice, "He giveth his beloved sleep"; then, "I am not beloved!" I would sing a hymn in a low voice sometimes, which seemed to soothe him and made him doze a little.

One day he called for Mr. Belflowers, saying he wanted to see him alone, and every one went out, and it must have been nearly an hour before Mr. Belflowers came out. Papa asked me to read to him from the Bible, and that always seemed a comfort to him. The 14th chapter of St. John was what he asked for most often: "Let not your heart be troubled." One day I was reading it to him when his niece, Mrs. Weston, came in, and I asked her to read it, and she took the Bible from me and read so beautifully. I saw at once how it comforted him, so slowly, so quietly, so distinctly, so impersonally. It might have been the blessed Saviour himself uttering those great words of comfort and promise to his disciples. The mind of a suffering, dying person acts slowly. If you hurry the words they cannot follow them without painful effort. When Cousin Lizzie got to the end of the chapter papa gasped out, "Go on, Elizabeth," and she went slowly on a long time.

The breathing became more and more terrible every hour, such a struggle that I could not endure to see it and be helpless to aid in any way. I would kneel beside the bed and take his hand and he would press mine in a grip which showed his pain, and at last as I knelt there I gave him up and prayed God to relieve him from his agony. Poor mamma could scarcely stay in the room, it was such an agony to her. She came in and knelt beside him and held his hand, and then she had to go out. But at last we all felt the end was at hand, and knelt beside the bed, praying for him with all our being, when he lifted his right hand

[205]

with a powerful sweep and said in a strong voice: "Lord, let me pass!" And it was all over in a few seconds, with no struggle or distress. It was peace after the awful storm, and we felt he was safely in the haven.

I had not slept for days and nights and went into the next room and fell into a deep sleep for an hour. When I woke I went into papa's room. The big bed had been moved out, and there he lay on the little single mahogany bed,* looking oh so peaceful and so beautiful; all the lines of care and anxiety gone and a look of youth and calm strength in his face. Oh, the comfort of that look. Mamma was sitting there, quite self-controlled and calm. I called her outside, for we had to make all the arrangements and give all the directions.

In the country there are no officials trained to take charge of things, and I suggested that we have Mr. Belflowers come and give him necessary directions. He was waiting down-stairs, and came up at once. Mamma began to tell him what she thought he had better do, but faltered and said: "I really don't know what directions to give!"

* I always sleep on that bed myself now.

He said: "There is no need for you to give any or to think about it, Mrs. Allston. The governor called me in three days ago and gave me every direction. He had it all in his mind, but his speech was so cut short by his breath that it took a good while for him to tell me. He told me what carpenters must make the coffin, where the specially selected and seasoned wood was; what negro was to drive the wagon which carried him and which horses; what horses to go in your carriage, with Aleck driving; who was to carry the invitation to the funeral, and with what horses on this side of the river, and to Georgetown, and what man was to take the boat and take it to Waccamaw. He said he wanted to be laid in the graveyard of Prince Frederick's church, as it was so near, and it would give too much trouble to be taken to Georgetown, and that after the war was over he could be moved to the family enclosure in Georgetown. And, ma'am, I have already given all the orders, just as he told me."

It is impossible to give any idea of the immense relief this was to mamma and to me. It just seemed a horror to see after all the sordid, terrible details. Papa had told John Locust and Stephen just how to arrange and dress and lay him out, so John had asked mamma to leave the room when the spirit had fled, and called her back when it was all done. The day before the end mamma had wanted to ask him some questions as to what she should do, etc. She broke down and said: "What can I ever do without you? Tell me what to do!" He pressed her hand and said: "The Lord will provide; have no fear." He could not direct her as to anything ahead in those troublous, changing times, but he could see that she was spared all trouble at the last, and we both felt it was the most touching and wonderful proof of his devotion even in the agony of death.

He was laid to rest in the churchyard of Prince Frederick's, just a mile away, where the beautiful half-finished brick church in whose building he had been so much interested, stood, a monument to war. All the trimmings and furnishings had been ordered in England, and, in running the blockade, they had been sunk. The architect, whose name was Gunn, had died, and was buried near the church, and the roofless but beautiful building stood there forlorn. There we laid him, with all the beauty of the wild spring flowers and growth he so loved around him, nearly under a big dogwood-tree in all its white glory. Crying and lamentation of the negroes who flocked along the road behind the wagon which carried papa, and filled the large graveyard, standing at a little distance behind the family, according to their rank and station on the plantation. Those who dug the grave had been specially named by papa, and it was considered a great honor. My dear father, if love could avail, when he reached those gates of pearl, they would fly open at his approach, for he carried the love and devotion of many people of all colors and classes.

As soon as possible my uncle, Chancellor Lesesne, arrived and opened and read the will. Mamma was named executrix and Chancellor Henry D. Lesesne executor. The house in Charleston and all the furniture were left to mamma, with all the house-servants and their families, and what carriages and horses she wanted, and a sum of money. To each of us five children a plantation and negroes, one hundred each. They were all named for each one. Charley was to have Chicora Wood, where we had always lived, and all the negroes who lived there. Brother Guendalos, the plantation adjoining on the south; Jane, Ditchfield, the plantation adjoining Chicora on the north; and to me was left Exchange, the plantation just north of that. To my sister Adèle, Waterford, a plantation on the Waccamaw, very valuable, and which would sell well; and Nightingale Hall, which was considered the place which would sell best, as it was at the pitch of tide most considered, being subject neither to freshet from above nor salt from the ocean below, was to be sold for the benefit of the heirs.

Then came an immense deal of writing and work for me. My brothers not being available nor any clerical outside help, I did all the writing and copying of the will to be sent round to the different heirs, and the lists of negroes, cattle, farm implements, and personal property, and helped Uncle Henry in every way. I have by me now the list of 600 negroes.

It was a great relief to have the work to do, for more and more as the days went on and the sense of thankfulness for his relief from suffering grew fainter, the sense of terrible desolation and sorrow possessed me. Papa was the only person in the world in whom I had absolute faith and confidence. I had never seen him show a trace of weakness or indecision. I had never seen him unjust or hasty in his judgment of a person. I had watched him closely and yet I had never seen him give way to temper or irritation, though I had

[210]

seen him greatly tried. Never a sign of self-indulgence, or indolence, or selfishness. It was my misfortune to see people's weaknesses with uncanny clearness, and my mother often rebuked me for being censorious and severe in my judgments of all around me; but never had I seen a thing in my father which I would criticise or wish to change. Only, I often wished he would talk more; but when I once said that very shyly to him, he laughed and said: "Child, when I have something to say I say it, and it seems to me that is a good plan."

We returned to Society Hill in May, mamma and I driving up in the carriage as we had gone down; but oh, how different the whole world was to us! The beauty of nature on the way, the woods in all the glory of their fresh leafage, the wild flowers, the birds, the gorgeous sunshine — all, all seemed a mockery. Our life was to be a gray, dull drab always. We stopped a night on the way up with kind, devoted friends, General Harllee and his charming wife, in their beautiful home, with a wonderful flower-garden. There was no power left in me to admire even, much less to enjoy. I had always been the most enthusiastic person in the world, too much so for polite standards. Now it was all gone. I was just a very thin, under-

sized, plain, commonplace young person, ready to
do anything I was told, but without one spark of
initiative. Mamma was crushed not only by her
grief but by the feeling that she was utterly inadequate to the task before her, that of looking
after and providing for over 600 negroes in this
time of war and stress, of seeing that the proper
supplies of food were at the different points where
they were needed.

Mamma had never had the least planning about
supplies, beyond buying her own groceries. The
supplies of rice, grist, potatoes, everything, had
been brought to her storeroom door regularly once
a week, calling for no thought on her part. Now
suddenly she had to plan and arrange for the 100
people on the farms in North Carolina, as well as
for the 500 down on the plantations. It was perfectly wonderful to see how she rose to the require-
ments of the moment, and how strong and level
her mind was. In a little while she had grasped
the full extent of the situation, and was perfectly
equal to her new position.

ADÈLE ALLSTON (later Mrs Arnoldus Van der Horst) and her uncle **JAMES LOUIS PETTIGRU**.

MRS. JOHN JULIUS PRINGLE AT "CHICORA WOOD."
The author, née Elizabeth Waties Allston, is shown in her old age at the family plantation where so much of her life was spent.

CHAPTER XIX

LOCH ADÈLE

SOON after we returned to Crowley Hill she determined to go to the North Carolina farms and see the people, so as to reassure them as to her taking care of them fully.

We started very early in the morning, Daddy Aleck driving, with baskets packed with lunch for the day and provisions to cook, for we expected to stay three or four days. The drive of thirty miles was charming until it got too hot, and we stopped under a tree by a spring, took out the horses and tied them in the shade and had our lunch, and rested until it became a little cooler. Loch Adèle, as we girls had named the farm, was a very pretty place with a mill and large pond, which we dignified into a loch, much to papa's amusement. A pretty rolling country, and the Pee Dee River, called the Yadkin as soon as it passed the line from South to North Carolina, ran a small rocky stream about a mile from the rambling farmhouse. Flats had brought supplies in large quantities up the river from Chicora, and most of the Charleston furniture had been brought by rail to Cheraw, fifteen miles away, and hauled out to this place, so that the house was thoroughly furnished, pictures hanging on the walls, because it seemed better than to keep them packed. The two lovely bas-reliefs of Thorwaldsen's, "Night" and "Morning," looked especially beautiful hanging on the white walls of the drawing-room, and the whole place was homelike and delightful with our Charleston belongings. And the poor negroes were so glad to see us and to realize that "Miss" was going to look after them and to the best of her ability take "Maussa's" place. They wanted to hear all about papa's illness and death and the funeral, and who had been honored by taking special place in it. Mamma was interviewed by each one separately, and had to repeat all the details over and over. She was very patient, to my great surprise, and, I think, to the people's, too, for she had never been as willing to listen to their long rigmaroles as papa had been. But now she listened to all and consoled them and wept with them over their mutual loss. Altogether the visit did us both good.

Old Daddy Hamedy, who was head man on the place, had been a first-class carpenter and still was, but when there was needed some one to take supervision of the farm and people up there, papa chose him on account of his character and intelligence. Papa had engaged a white man, a Mr. Yates, who lived some miles away, to give an eye to the place from time to time and write him how things went on, and Hamedy was to apply to Mr. Yates if anything went wrong. He was originally from the North, but he had bought a farm near the little town of Morven some years before, and lived here ever since. Mamma sent to ask Mr. Yates to come and see her, and he came. He was a very smart man, but impressed me most unpleasantly as unreliable and unscrupulous, as I watched him talking to mamma. He evidently felt that, papa being gone, his time had come, and was quite sure he could manage my mother easily. He was most flattering in his admiration, which was not surprising, for my mother was beautiful in her plain black frock and widow's cap.

In trying to make easy conversation as he sat and talked to us, he asked: "Miss Allston, do you smoke?"

In some surprise my mother answered: "No, I have never smoked."

"Well, well," he said. "You wouldn't find

[215]

another lady of your age in this country that didn't smoke."

This nearly upset my gravity, for the idea of my mother's smoking was too much for me, and I went out down to the mill-pond. Into this lake my father had had rolled many hogsheads packed securely with bottles of old Madeira wine, as being the best chance of saving them from the Yankees. They were certainly not safe at Chicora Wood, only about twenty miles from the mouth of Winyah Bay, when gunboats could run up from the sea so easily. So the wine was packed and shipped by his flats in charge of faithful men. I remember when the flats were going, on one occasion, papa wanted to send up a very beautiful marble group of "The Prodigal Son," which was always in the drawing-room at Chicora, and he called in Joe Washington, who was to take charge of the flat, to look at it, and told him that he would have it carefully packed by the carpenter, and he wanted him to be specially careful of it; whereupon Joe said:

"Please, sir, don't have it pack. I'll tek good kere of it, but please lef it so en I kin look at it en enjoy it. I'll neber let nuthin' hut it."

So papa acceded and did not have it packed,

and on that open flat, amid barrels and boxes and propelled by oars and poles, only a little shed at one end under which the eight hands could take shelter in case of rain, "The Prodigal Son" and the happy father made their journey of 300 miles in perfect safety. And I may say here the group was brought back when the war was over, and now rests in the old place in the drawing-room at Chicora Wood. How it escaped Sherman I do not know; some one must have hid it in the woods.

CHAPTER XX

SHADOWS

I INSERT here an extract from my diary:

"Croley Hill, Sunday July 19th, 1864. Just as we were leaving for Church the paper came and there in it was the dreadful intelligence that my cousin Gen'l Johnston Pettigrew, who was wounded on the 17th had died of his wounds. It is too dreadful! If I could I would hope that this, like the first might be a false report, but something tells me it is true. . . . Next to Uncle (James L. Petigru) he was the light of the family, so clever, so learned, so noble; and how I have almost adored him in his nobleness and wisdom; how I have sat and listened to Uncle and himself talking until I thought nothing could ever be as brilliant and pleasant as that; but now both have gone and we shall never see their equals again. . . . I am glad I have Cousin Johnston's beautiful book 'Spain and the Spaniards' which he gave me. We heard he was wounded at Gettysburg but his name was not mentioned among the generals and never since, so we supposed it was a mistake, and *Now . . .*" This was a terrible blow and distress. After this, sad news kept coming in of reverses, and things looked dark. The hospitals were in great need of stimulants and mamma determined to send the rye she had made to the still about twenty miles away and have it made into whiskey. Daddy Aleck took it and told of the dangers he had encountered on the way, so that when it was finished, he was afraid to go for it alone, and mamma told Jinty and me we must ride along with him.

About this time my cousin, Captain Phil Porcher, of the navy, went out on a little vessel, the *Juno*, which had been built in Charleston harbor to run the blockade, and nothing was ever heard of him or of any of the crew or officers. Weeks passed into months and not a word of the fate of the boat. It was terrible for Aunt Louise and her daughters. Mamma wrote and begged them to come and stay with us, and they came. It was dreadful to see their sufferings. My aunt was a beautiful and heroic figure. They would not act as though they had heard of his death, for each day there was the hope that when the paper came there would be some news of him. They tried so hard to be cheerful and hope against hope.

But no news ever did come. It remains one of the mysteries of the deep.*

Phil Porcher was a gallant, charming, and exemplary man, and the greatest loss to the whole family and to the country.

* Since writing this my esteemed friend, Professor Yates Snowden, has given me an interesting account of an interview with Mr. B——, a pilot of Charleston, who was one of two men who were picked up on the coast of Georgia, survivors of the *Juno*. They had spent days on a chicken-coop in the terrible storm which wrecked the overloaded little boat.

CHAPTER XXI

PREPARING TO MEET SHERMAN

AFTER my aunt and cousins left we began to bury every treasure we had. All the silver which had not been sent to Morven was packed in a wooden chest, and Mr. William Evans, our nearest neighbor, came one day in his wagon to take it as, it was supposed, to the station to send it away by the railroad. Nelson went with him, and they drove by a winding route into some very thick woods near, and Nelson dug a deep hole and the two of them lowered it in with ropes, filled the grave, and marked the spot. That was one weight off of our minds. We kept just enough for daily use. I became an expert in burying. Three sheets were a necessity; one to put the top earth on, with moss and leaves and everything to look natural, then one to put the second colored earth near the surface, and one to put every grain of the yellow clay below, one little pellet of which would tell the tale that a hole had been dug.

Charley came home for a few days on his way

to Virginia, the boys at the Arsenal having been called out. He was just sixteen, and it was pitiful to see him weighed down by his knapsack and all the heavy things he had to march with, for he was very thin and gaunt. Mamma consulted him as to what to do with the old Madeira, of which she still had a good deal packed in barrels in the storeroom. He consulted Nelson, and they agreed to pack it in the big piano box, which was still used as a grain bin. So the piano box was cleared out and emptied, and brought into the little front porch, which it nearly filled, as there had been a room cut off from each end of the porch, which originally ran the length of the house, and this left this porch with steps all the way along down to the ground, only about five steps. Here they brought hay and we all helped bring the bottles of wine up quietly from the storeroom, and Nelson, who was an expert, packed them beautifully. It was done so quietly that the servants in the yard knew nothing of it. We all went to bed at the usual hour, but at twelve o'clock Charley and Nelson got up, having provided ropes, spades, and everything necessary in one of the shed-rooms, which Charley occupied, also two pieces of round oak as rollers. They dug a hole big enough for the piano box, using sheets for the earth, as I have described, and how those two accomplished it is a mystery, without help, but they did put that huge box into that deep hole, covered it up, removing the dirt which was too much, and levelled the surface, raked the whole front road, and then brought the wagon and rolled it back and forth over it, making it look natural; so that in the morning there was no trace of anything unusual. Charley left the next day for Virginia, and oh, how miserable we were! Poor mamma, he was her special darling, named after her youngest brother, who gave his life for his friend so long ago.

Mamma was kept very busy, sending supplies in different directions, and having cloth spun and woven. She sent demijohns of whiskey to the hospitals and some down to Mr. Belflowers for use on the plantation in case of sickness (the darkies having a feeling that no woman can be safely delivered of a child without a liberal supply of whiskey).

I cannot mark the passage of time exactly, but the report came that Sherman was advancing, and there came awful rumors of what he was doing and would do. We made long homespun bags, quite narrow, and with a strong waistband, and a strong button, to be worn under the skirts. And into these we put all our treasures. They said every photograph was destroyed, after great indignities. I took all my photos of my dear ones (such sights they look now, but then seemed beautiful). I put them one by one in a basin of clear cold water and left them a few minutes, when I found I could peal them off of the card; and then I pasted them into a little book which I could carry in one of my pockets. The book was Brother's passport-book when he was travelling abroad, and I have it now with all the pictures in it. Our kind and generous neighbor, Mrs. Wm. Evans, was a very, very thin, tall woman, but when I ran over to see her during these days of anxiety and she came out into the piazza to meet me, I could not believe my eyes. She seemed to be an enormously stout woman! I looked so startled that she said:

"My dear Bessie, they say these brutes take everything but what you have on and burn it before your eyes. So I have bags of supplies, rice and wheat flour and sugar and what little coffee we had, hung round my waist, and then I have on all the clothes I can possibly stand, three dresses for one item." And then we both laughed until

[224]

we nearly fell from exhaustion. And when I ran home and told mamma we had another great laugh, and oh, it was such a mercy to have a good hearty laugh in those days of gloom and anxiety. We never quite got to Mrs. Evans's condition, but we each had treasures unknown to the others concealed about us.

Things in the Confederacy were going worse and worse. It was an agony to read the papers. My sister, Mrs. Van der Horst, came home from Wilmington, bringing her maid, Margaret. Her husband did not think it safe for her to stay any longer there. It was a great comfort to have her with us. The Yankees were reported nearer and nearer, but we never saw any one to hear positively where they were. Then one evening, just at dusk, two horsemen galloped up to the front door, tied their horses and came in. They were Charleston Light Dragoons acting as scouts for General Hampton — Julius Pringle and Tom Ferguson. They came to tell us Hampton was protecting all our troops as they left the State. They were the very last, and Mr. Pringle said to mamma:

"I knew you had wine and whiskey in the house and I came to beg you for God's sake to destroy it all. Do not let a drop be found in the house, I implore you."

Mamma said: "But, Julius, I have not sent all that whiskey to the hospitals yet, and it is so greatly needed! I have two demijohns still."

"Oh, Mrs. Allston, I implore you, do not hesitate. Have those demijohns broken to pieces the first thing to-morrow morning."

She promised. We gave them a good supper, of which they were in great need. Nelson fed the horses. They took two hours' sleep and then left in the middle of the night. As they were going, there were shots heard on the public road which ran back of our house about 400 yards. The two dragoons jumped on their horses and galloped off from the front door into the darkness of the night. It was an awful moment. They were gone, our last friends and protectors, and the agony in Mr. Pringle's face was indescribable.

We found the next morning that the shots had been the forerunners only of the license we had to expect. It was negroes shooting our hogs, which were fat and tempting. Early the next morning mamma called Nelson and Daddy Aleck and had them bring the wheelbarrow and put into it the demijohns with the precious rye whiskey and roll them to a little stream near by, and pour it into the water. We went along and it was a melancholy procession, and Daddy Aleck secretly wept and openly grumbled, as he felt he had risked his life for that whiskey. As it was poured into the branch by Nelson, who also loved whiskey, Daddy Aleck went lower down the stream and knelt down and drank as if he were a four-footed beast. Then we went back and wondered how we could dispose of the two dozen bottles of wine still in the storeroom. Papa had once said it might prove the most salable thing we had after the war. I undertook to conceal them, and, going up into the garret, I found the flooring was not nailed down, and, lifting one board at a time, I laid the bottles softly in, softly because they were placed on the ceiling laths and it was an old house. But the ceiling held and the bottles were disposed of.

After having done all he could to help mamma that day, Nelson came to her and said: "Miss, I want you to give me some provision and let me go for a while."

She exclaimed: "Nelson, you cannot leave us when these Yankees are coming! You must not leave us unprotected."

He said: "Miss, I know too much. Ef dem Yankee was to put a pistol to my head and say tell what you know or I'll shoot you, I cudn't trust meself. I dunno what I mite do! Le' me go, miss." So mamma put up his bag of provisions and he went.

The next day she decided it was best to send Daddy Aleck off, as he said if she let him go he thought he could take the horses in the swamp and save them. So he went, taking the horses and a bag of harness and all the saddles. It was a brave, clever thing of the old man to carry out. But we felt truly desolate when both he and Nelson were gone, and we only had Phibby and Margaret, Della's maid, and Nellie, Nelson's wife, and little Andrew, who was a kind of little dwarf, a very smart and competent, well-trained dining-room servant, who looked about fourteen but was said to be over twenty.

CHAPTER XXII

THEY COME!

AS everything would be seized by the enemy when they came, we lived very high, and the things which had been preciously hoarded until the men of the family should come home were now eaten. Every day we had a real Christmas dinner; all the turkeys and hams were used. One day mamma had just helped us all to a delicious piece of turkey when Phibby rushed in, crying: "Miss, dey cumin!" Bruno, Jane's little water-spaniel, began to bark, and she rushed out to the wide roofless porch where he was, threw her arms round his neck and held his throat so tight he couldn't bark, just as a soldier was about to strike him with a sword. I was terrified for her as she knelt there in the middle of the porch, holding him; but they only looked down at her, as they rushed by on each side into the house, calling out:

"Whiskey! We want liquor! Don't lie; we know you have it! We want whiskey! We want firearms!" Each one said the same thing.

Mamma was very calm. As they clamored she

said: "You may search the house. You will find none. I had some whiskey, but it is here no longer."

They seemed delighted at the sight of the dinner-table, and for a time were occupied eating and pocketing all that could be pocketed. When the renewed cry for wine, whiskey, and firearms came, mamma took from the nail where it hung the huge storeroom key, and went down the steps to the storeroom, just in time to prevent its being smashed in with an axe. She opened the door and they rushed in with many insulting words. Poor Phibby was wild with terror, and followed mamma, closely holding on to her skirt and entreating her not to go.

"Miss, dem'll kill yu, fu Gawd sake don' go wid dem." But mamma showed no sign of excitement or alarm and never seemed to hear the dreadful things they said. They opened box after box in vain, but at last in the box under all the rest they came on a bottle and the men shouted: "We knew you were lying!" The finder struck the head off with one blow, and, putting the bottle to his mouth, took a long draft. Then there was a splutter and choking, and he got rid of it as quickly as possible, to the amusement and joy of the others, who had envied his find. It was our one treasured bottle of olive-oil, which had been put out of reach, to be kept for some great occasion.

Upstairs in her bedroom my sister was having a trying time. She unlocked her trunk to prevent its being ripped open with a sword, and looked on while they ran through it, taking all her jewels and everything of value, holding up each garment for examination and asking its uses, each one being greeted by shouts of laughter. She, having recently come, had not concealed or buried any of her things. After disposing of her big trunk, they turned to a closet, where a man's leather trunk was. They asked for the key, and when she said she did not have it, they cut it open, and there on top lay a sword. Then there were howls of: "We knew you were lying. You said you had no arms." Della only answered: "I did not know what was in this trunk." It was her brother-in-law Lewis Van der Horst's trunk. He had been killed fighting gallantly in Virginia, and his trunk had been sent home by his friends to his brother without the key.

All this time I was with another party, who were searching for liquor, and I followed them into the garret. It was odd how impossible it was not to follow them and see what they did. I was told afterward that in most places the women shut themselves up in a room while they searched the house; but, with us, we were irresistibly borne to keep up with them and watch them. When I heard them tramping over the garret, the loose boards rattling, I flew up myself and stood there while they opened every box and trunk, taking anything of any value, every now and then quarrelling over who should have a thing. I was in misery, for the boards seemed to be crying aloud: "Take us up and you'll find something. Take us up." Whenever they asked me anything I answered with some quick, sharp speech which would intensely amuse any one but the questioner, who generally relapsed into sulky silence. They seemed to be in great dread of being surprised by Hampton's cavalry, whom they spoke of as "the devil, for you never knew where he was," so they did everything very rapidly.

All this time there were parties going all over the yard, running ramrods into the ground to find buried things. My terror about that big box of wine was intense as I saw them. They even went under the big piazza at the back of the house and rammed every foot of the earth. It was a marvel that they never thought of coming to the front, having come up at the back of the house from the public road. They never even opened the gate which separated the front yard from the back, and so the great piano box was never found. Little Andrew we never had felt very sure of, and so everything about the burying of things was kept from him. As they left, Margaret and Nellie came in crying bitterly. They had taken every trinket and treasure they had, and all their warm clothes. Margaret was specially loud in her denunciation:

"I always bin hear dat de Yankees was gwine help de nigger! W'a' kynd a help yu call dis! Tek ebery ting I got in de wurld, my t'ree gold broach," etc., etc. Poor Margaret had sometimes been supposed to be light-fingered, and she had returned from Wilmington with a good deal of jewelry, which we wondered about; but now, poor soul, it was all gone. For four days the army kept passing along that road, and we heard shouts and shots and drums beating, and every moment expected another visit, but, as I said, they moved in haste, always fearing to leave the main road and be ambushed by Hampton's ubiquitous scouts.

[233]

We never went to bed or took off our clothes during that time. We sat fully dressed in the parlor, all night through, Phibby always sitting with us on the floor near the door, leaning straight up against the wall, her legs stretched out in front of her, nodding and praying. She was a great comfort. Mamma tried to induce her to go to bed and sleep, saying:

"Phœbe, you have nothing to fear. They won't hurt you."

All her answer was: "Miss, yu tink I gwine lef' yu fu dem weeked men fu kill, no ma'am, not Phibby. I'll stay right here en pertect yu."

Mamma read calmly. Della slept on the sofa. I scribbled in my journal. I will make a little extract here from the little paper book I carried in my pocket. It seems very trivial and foolish; but here it is:

"March 8th, 1865. — Twelve o'clock! and we still sit whispering around the fire, Phœbe on the floor nodding, Della with her feet extended trying to rest on the sofa, and I on a stool scribbling, scribbling to while away the time till dawn. Thank God, one more quiet day, and we so hoped for a quiet night, but a little after nine Phœbe ran in saying she heard them coming. Oh, the

chill and terror that ran through me when I heard
that; but it proved a false alarm. . . . I never
fully understood terror until now, and yet every
one says our experience of them is mild. . . .
They delight in making terrible threats of ven-
geance and seem to gloat over our misery. Yesterday a captain was here who pretended to be
all kindness and sympathy over the treatment we
had received from the foragers. . . . He did not
enter the house. We placed a chair on the piazza
and gave him what we had to eat. But when he
began to talk, he seemed almost worse than any
other. He vowed never to take a prisoner, said
he would delight in shooting down a rebel prisoner
and often did it! My disgust was intense, but I
struggled hard to keep cool and succeeded somewhat. He asked, 'Do you know what you are
fighting for?' I replied, 'Existence.' He said,
'We won't let you have it,' with such a grin. . . .
He said, 'At the beginning of this war, I didn't
care a cent about a nigger, but I'd rather fight for
ten years longer than let the South have her inde-
pendence.' Then, with a chuckle, he said, 'But
we'll starve you out, not in one place that we have
visited have we left *three meals*.' At something
Della said he exclaimed, 'Oh, I know what you

mean, you mean the Almighty, but the Almighty has got nothing to do with this war.' Such blasphemy silenced us completely."

The tales the negroes heard from one another were terrific, as to what the Yankees had done, and what the negroes had done. We never saw any one during this time but those in the yard. Little Andrew, whom we never had felt sure of, behaved very well. We had thought he would probably go off with the Yankees, but whether his experience of them had not been such as to make him desire a closer knowledge I don't know, but certainly no one could have behaved better than he did, laying the table with the few forks and spoons mamma had managed to hide, and bringing in our scanty meals with as much dignity as if things were unchanged; and he was a help, though he never expressed devotion or the contrary, only brought in specially hair-raising stories of the outrages committed on every side, many of which stories proved to have no foundation in fact.

At last the noises on the highway ceased, and we knew Sherman's great army had passed on toward the North.

We began to breathe freely and feel that we could go to bed at night and sleep. At first we went to bed with all our clothes on, but gradually we realized that the army had passed entirely, leaving no troops in the country behind them. News began to come in, and we knew that Sherman had burned Columbia and left a trail of desolation where he had passed. The fear of the Confederate troops had kept them to a narrow strip of country. It was like the path stripped by a tornado, narrow but complete destruction in it. Mrs. Evans ventured over to make us a visit. She had not yet assumed her natural proportions, but had lightened her burden so that she could walk the half-mile between our houses. We were eager to hear her experiences, but, to her intense disappointment, she had had none! She had not seen a Yankee! It shows how careful they were not to leave the main road for fear of ambush. She had prepared many brilliant, severe speeches to make to them, for she had a very witty, sharp tongue and was as bold as a lion, so that she felt very sore and aggrieved, and when she heard of our experiences her blood boiled that we had not lashed them with bitter words.

About four days after they passed Daddy Aleck reappeared with the horses, safe and sound, but greatly distressed that he had waked hearing shots near one morning, packed up his things quickly on his horses, and taken them deeper in the swamp and left one of the side-saddles hanging on a limb. Nelson also arrived, looking weary and blanched by his experiences. Daddy Aleck was a naturally brave, combative nature and very tough, but Nelson was a lover of peace and comfort, and camping out in the swamp was no joy to him. He and Daddy Aleck were never friends and distrusted each other, so they had not cared to go together.

CHAPTER XXIII

DADDY HAMEDY'S APPEAL — IN THE TRACK OF SHERMAN'S ARMY

ONLY a few days after Daddy Aleck's and Nelson's return, Brutus came from Loch Adèle, bearing a piece of paper with hieroglyphics on it in pencil. After much studying over it by each one of us, we found it was a note from dear, faithful Daddy Hamedy: "Miss, cum at once. Mister Yates dun dribe de peeple." Then mamma questioned the boy, not telling what trouble we had to make out the important document of which he was the bearer. He told his story. General Kilpatrick and the whole army had camped on the place a week. They had burned the gin-house after taking all the provisions they could carry away, and left the negroes without a thing to eat, and the whole country was the same — nothing to eat for the white people who belonged there any more than for them — and Mr. Yates had come to the farm the day before and told Daddy Hamedy they must all leave the country at once and go back down to the low country from which they came. Daddy

Hamedy had answered him civilly; he said it would take them a day to prepare, and as soon as Mr. Yates left he had started this runner, Brutus, off. He had travelled all night to bring it quick! Mamma praised him and gave him the best meal she could and told him to go to sleep. Everything was stirring that night, preparing for an early start. Mamma went over to see Mr. Evans and consulted him about it and told him she was going up the next day. He advised her greatly against it, but, finding he could not persuade her to give it up, he said he would ride on horseback along with us. He had saved his riding-horse by taking it in the swamp as Daddy Aleck had.

So at daylight the next morning we started; mamma and I in the carriage with a basket of cooked food, Daddy Aleck driving and Brutus beside him on the box, Mr. Evans riding beside the carriage. It was an awful experience, as it must always be to travel in the track of a destroying army. To begin with, the road was a quagmire. It took an experienced driver like Daddy Aleck to get us through, and even with all his care Brutus and Mr. Evans had often to get a rail from the fences along the road and pry our wheels out of the bog. We were never out of the sight of dead things, and the stench was almost unbearable. Dead horses all along the way and, here and there, a leg or an arm sticking out of a hastily made too-shallow grave. Along the way ten cows dead in one pen, and then eight or ten calves dead in another. Dead hogs everywhere; the effort being to starve the inhabitants out, no living thing was left in a very abundant country. It is a country of small farms, just two-roomed houses; all now tightly shut up, no sign of life. Wells with all means of drawing water destroyed. We stopped at one or two houses and knocked without any response, but at last we knocked at one where a tall, pale woman opened a crack of the door wide enough to talk through. No, she had nothing; could not help us in any way to draw water. So Daddy Aleck got his halters and tied them together and let his horse-bucket down into the well, and I was so thirsty I drank, but mamma would not. As we got beyond Cheraw, fifteen miles on our way, we began to meet some of our people from Morven, who had started on their hundred-mile flight to the low country, in obedience to Mr. Yates's mandate — forlorn figures, a pot sometimes balanced on the head, and a bundle of clothing swung on the back, a baby in arms,

[241]

sometimes one or two children trailing behind. Mamma stopped as we got to each traveller and told them to turn back; she had come to feed them and do all she could for them, and they need have no fear. To Daddy Aleck's great indignation, she took some of the impedimenta from the most heavily loaded and we went on our way. We had made such an early start that few had gone more than a few miles, and all were so rejoiced to see mamma and so thankful to turn back that we began to feel quite cheerful.

It was lucky, for things were worse and worse as we went on; and when finally we got to pretty Loch Adèle a scene of desolation met us — every animal killed, and the negroes had had a kind of superstitious feeling about making use of the meat, or they could have cured meat enough to last the winter; for, though the Yankees had burned down the gin-house, with cotton and provisions and salt, they could not destroy the latter, and there, in a blackened mass, was a small mountain of salt. If Mr. Yates had been any good he could have seen to that. The house was not burned, but everything in it was broken to pieces — beds, sideboard, chairs, tables, and on the floor the fragments of the beautiful big medallions of "Night" and "Morning," chopped into little pieces. I found one baby's foot, whole, in the mass of rubbish, which I kept a long time, it was so beautiful, quite the size of a real baby's.

We had a tremendous afternoon's work to clear away and make the place habitable for the night, but Brutus worked with me and I got two women to help, and we managed to prop up a table and put boards over the bottomless chairs, and by supper-time, with a bright fire burning, for we had only brought two candles, it was quite a different-looking place. Mamma had brought two roast chickens and a piece of boiled bacon (as she had buried a box of bacon, fortunately) and a loaf of bread and some corn-dodgers which we toasted by the fire, so we had a good supper. The thing that worried us most was the fixing a comfortable bed for Mr. Evans, but we succeeded in propping up things, and, putting some straw and the blankets we had brought, made a comfortable resting-place; but, when it was all fixed, Mr. Evans absolutely refused to occupy it, said he preferred to rest on the three-legged sofa by the fire, and insisted that mamma and I should take the bed. Which, after a little friendly contention, we did, and most thankful was I to stretch myself on anything after the fatigues and agitations of the day.

Early in the morning we were up and busy. Brutus cooked hominy for breakfast and fried some bacon. After breakfast Mr. Evans, seeing mamma equal to the situation, rode back home. Before we had sat down, forlorn-looking country people began to arrive. They sat around the fire on broken chairs while we ate breakfast. Then Mr. Yates arrived. He was so startled when he saw mamma he looked as though he would faint. He said good morning and then went out. People still came and mamma was filled with wonder as to what it meant, till one man said:

"Wall, when's the auction goin' to begin?"

Mamma said: "What auction?"

He said: "We was notified by your agent how as there was to be an auction here to-day, an' everything on the place was to be sold. I come to buy a plough."

Mamma said: "There will be no auction here to-day."

Then they one by one rose and said: "I reckon if there ain't to be no auction, we better be gittin' home." And they made their adieus and left.

Then we understood. Mr. Yates had ordered the negroes to leave, and intended to sell out all the things on the place and take the money, never supposing there was any possibility of mamma's being informed in time to get up to prevent it. But he reckoned without knowing the negroes or mamma. As soon as they had all left, she summoned Mr. Yates and had a talk with him. She told him she would not need his services any more, that he had quite exceeded his authority in sending the negroes off without consulting her, and that the fact of his having advertised an auction without her consent also showed that he misunderstood the situation. He was quite insolent and said he would not go unless he was paid in full. To which she answered she had no intention of letting him go unpaid, asked for his accounts, looked over them, and gave him a check on Mr. Malloy in Cheraw.

Mamma found that below the salt was a large pile of rough rice which would not burn, and which was ample provision for the negroes. On examination we found that only the outside of the pile of rough rice was scorched. Rough rice (which is the rice still encased in its thick, rough, outer shell) cannot burn, and there was enough rice there to keep the people well fed a long time, and they prefer rice to any other food. They beat it in mortars made by taking about three feet of the trunk of a hardwood-tree and burning out the centre, so as to hold about six quarts of grain. Then they make a pestle from a smaller limb of hardwood neatly smoothed and rounded at the end; and with these crude implements the stiff, hard, almost indestructible hull is easily removed.

Mamma also found that away from the path of the enemy there were supplies of sorghum syrup and potatoes, etc., which people would gladly bring to exchange for salt and rice. So we turned home, an immense load lifted from our hearts. The people would not really suffer!

Mamma made a little talk to the negroes, and told them just to stay quietly there and do their ordinary work, and that she had made arrangements for provisions for them to be brought to the farm every week, and that very soon she would have the flats come up from Chicora Wood and take them all back to the low country, and begged them not to lose their good reputation by breaking the law in any way, now that the whole country was so upset. And she thanked them for having behaved so well ever since papa had been taken, and having made it easy for her by their good conduct. And they courtesied and said: "Tank Gawd" that she had come to "luk after"

her people and not let them be driven away by
"Po' buckra." Altogether it was a very com-
forting little scene. Daddy Hamedy made a little speech, assuring her of his fidelity to her, and
that he would look after everything and let her
know if anything went wrong. He apologized
much for not having been able to protect the property, but he said General Kilpatrick and the soldiers wouldn't listen to him at all, and just cut
the dam and drained off the water and got Maussa's wine, and got drunk on it, and sent some off
in wagons, and were so harsh to him he just had
to keep out of sight of them. By the time they
set fire to the gin-house, full of good provisions
and all the fine cotton-crop, he was struck down
by a severe chill and had to go to bed. And,
when one looked at his face, one had to believe in
his distress. Three of the young men had gone
off with the soldiers. They wanted to take many
more, but "tank de Lawd," they had more sense
than to go. We left early the next morning and
returned to Crowley.

CHAPTER XXIV

SHADOWS DEEPEN

AFTER this things are vague in my mind, only an impression of distress and gloom. I got a letter from my cousin and friend, Hal Lesesne, telling of the successive falling back which was so terrible to them all. He had been so long in the forts around Charleston, and so greatly desired to see active service in Virginia, and now, alas, things were so black, no one could help fearing. "But be assured," he said, "we are fighting every step of the way, and make the enemy pay dearly for their gain." When I got that letter he had already fallen, killed in the very last battle of the war, Averysboro, I think. This was a great sorrow to me; and the surrender was just crushing and numbing to all my being. Men began to come in on their way home from the front, worn, weary, gaunt, and hungry. They had lived days and days and fought on a handful of parched corn. Their shoes were worn out, their uniforms ragged; only their spirit was undimmed, and that made them suffer so in the sense of failure.

My dear brother Charley finally came, a ghost of his former self, shoulders bowed down by marching with his heavy knapsack. He looked so ill and changed, we were not surprised when we found he had typhoid fever. He had been taken in and kindly nursed by friends on his way home, but he was a pitiful sight.

CHAPTER XXV

GLEAMS OF LIGHT

THEN one day, to our amazement, Sam Galant came with two horses which he had brought back safe all the way from Virginia! They were thin and so was he, but it was a wonderful feat, without money and without food, at a time when the soldiers returning home on foot were desperate for a horse to till and cultivate the little farms to which they were returning empty-handed. How was it possible for Sam to escape capture by some of them, almost hopeless at the great distance from their homes, which they must travel mostly afoot! Sam had wonderful tales to tell of his experiences. He kept with Hampton's Cavalry all the time, leading horses to be at hand to replace those killed in battle. He gave a thrilling account of the death of Bill, the mail horse. Edward Wells, of the Charleston Light Dragoons, was riding him, and as they were galloping out of Cheraw, just over the bridge, a shell went through Bill from tail to head, without exploding, leaving Mr. Wells standing on his feet unhurt. "Sam, a horse," he called, and, according to Sam's tale, he stepped up instantly with a fresh horse, Mr. Wells mounted and was gone. Sam concluded:

"Yes, ma'am, Mr. Wells is the bravest man in the world, I believe. He neber mind de shell busting all 'round him, en I was dere right alongside him, ready to his han'."

Oh, if I had only got Sam to come and tell it all to me quietly long afterward, so that I could write it down as I did Daddy Ancrum's story! But Sam was comparatively young, some years younger than myself, and I always thought there was time. I never thought of his dying.

One day a messenger arrived from the plantation to mamma, with a badly scribbled line on brown paper: "Miss, cum quick, dem de 'stribute ebry ting." Mamma questioned the boy. He said the people had gone wild, that "a Capting from de Yankee A'my kum en a kerridge en tell de people dem is free en ebry ting belongst to dem. No wite peeple 'ill neber jum back, en den him 'stribute ebery ting."

Mamma told Daddy Aleck to have the carriage ready early the next morning, and she and I started off, leaving Della and Jane still at Crowley, with all the servants. Charley rode with us on horseback and, to our surprise, Julius Pringle turned up the evening before and said he would ride along with us too. The presence of these two, just home from all the dangers and suffering of the war, now here safe and sound, made the journey a great pleasure. Mr. Pringle rode Jerry, Charley's young half-Arab stallion, which mamma had sent on to Virginia for him, and which he rode as one of Hampton's scouts all the last year of the war. We had not gone far when a runner on foot from Chicora Wood met us.

He said: "Miss, I got a pa'tikler messidge fu yu, en I wan' to speak to yu private." So mamma got out of the carriage and went a little way into the woods with him. He said: "A'nt Milly say don't kum, 'tis dang'us, but ef yu does kum, don't keep de publik road. Dem de watch fu yu! Kum troo de 'oods." Mamma thanked and told him to go on to Crowley and rest and Miss Adèle would give him plenty to eat, and when he was rested, he could start back. She got into the carriage and we drove on.

I never have understood that message from Maum Milly, whether it was a genuine anxiety on her part, or whether it was to keep mamma from coming and asserting her rights, by intimidating

[252]

her. Maum Milly had always been greatly considered and trusted. She held herself and her
family as vastly superior to the ordinary run of
negroes, the aristocracy of the race. Whatever
her intention was, the message had no effect on
mamma's plans, and we never left the public road.

That night we stopped at a house where dark
caught us, and asked for shelter, simply that; we
had provisions. The family were from Georgetown and had refugeed here, the Sampsons, and
they received us with enthusiastic hospitality and
kindness, making us most comfortable for the
night, and giving us a delicious and abundant
supper and breakfast of fried chicken, so that we
were able to keep our supplies for the next day.
I do not think I ever saw as beautiful a young
Jewess as the daughter of the family, Deborah
Sampson.

When we got to Plantersville we drove to Mrs.
Weston to ask about them all, for we knew nothing of how they had fared in these dark days.
Cousin Lizzie was rejoiced to see us after all we
had both gone through, and Mr. Weston and herself and Pauline most hospitably invited us to
stay with them, until we could make arrangements to get the log house in order for us to

occupy, as it had been shut up a long time. There was so much to hear and so much to tell that it was hard to go to bed. They had been through a great trial in the Bunker raid, when this Yankee had come through the little village in an open carriage, followed by a throng of negroes, whooping and yelling with joy, in response to his announcement that they were free, and that everything belonged to them. He went to every house and seized every article of value, took the earrings from women's ears and the rings from their fingers; for the inhabitants of the little hamlet had been so far removed from the centre of war that they had not thought of concealing their valuables and jewelry, as no one had any fear of the negroes. This seems to me a wonderful tribute to them, and they deserve to have the changes rung on it. When this man, announcing himself as "A N'united State Officer," as they called it, authorized them to take possession of everything as their own, it is a marvel that license and shooting did not ensue on their part; for the end had not come yet, and none of the men had come home from the army. There were only women and children and two old men in the village, and there might have been frightful scenes there.

They took all Bunker gave them, but touched nothing themselves where the white owners were present. It was only on the plantations, where the owners were absent, that, on his persuasion, they pitched in and "stributed" the contents of the houses. That darky word for it is good, for each one took what he selected as fast as he could till there was nothing left.

The next day Mr. Pringle rode up with a note from his mother, asking us to go down and stay with her at the White House, their plantation, twelve miles south of Plantersville, on the Pee Dee River, — that is, the Pee Dee ran in front of the house, and the Black River half a mile away at the back. Mamma accepted the invitation with much pleasure. Mrs. Pringle and her husband and Mary had been in Europe when the war broke out. The sons, Julius, Poinsett, and Lynch, were at Heidelberg University. The young men at once left, ran the blockade, and entered the Confederate service. Mr. and Mrs. Pringle and Mary remained in Italy. Mr. Pringle died and was buried in the beautiful cemetery in Rome in 1863, and the next spring Mrs. Pringle and Mary came to America, and stayed with Fanny Butler (daughter of Fanny Kemble), at Butler Place, outside of

Philadelphia, until they were able to slip through the lines and get into Virginia, only to find the darling of them all, Poinsett, had been recently killed in battle. It was too awful for them. They stayed where they could occasionally see the other two boys, until this winter, when they made their way down to the plantation, to remain there.

I had never been to the White House before, though I had always heard of it as very beautiful; a picturesque, rambling house with three gables, set facing the river about 200 yards away, in a most beautiful garden, which had been planted by Mr. Poinsett, who was a specialist on gardens, a botanist. The White House was even more beautiful than I had imagined. As soon as you left the road you entered on a lane bordered on each side with most luxuriant climbing roses, now in riotous bloom, long garlands of white roses swaying in the breeze, high up, and quarrelling for supremacy with long garlands of pink roses. This lane took you direct to the Pee Dee River, where you made a sharp turn and drove along the avenue of live oaks just on the edge of the river, which had here a sand beach like the seashore. The effect was delightful; on the left the river, only a few feet away, on the right a green lawn, until you came to the vegetable-garden. A picture garden! All the vegetables sedately in straight rows, and having nothing to do with each other. The French artichokes standing in stately stiff rows, not so much as glancing at the waving asparagus bed, nor the rows of pale-green mammoth roses, which turn out to be heads of lettuce. I had never seen a vegetable-garden which was ornamental before. While I was taking it in we entered the flower-garden, with a wilderness of roses, azaleas, camellias, and other beautiful shrubs and plants.

Mamma and Mrs. Pringle were rejoiced to see each other, but it was sad, for both had suffered much sorrow since their last meeting. Papa had been taken from us and Mrs. Pringle had lost both her husband and beautiful son, so it was a long time before they could become composed. That evening, however, they made up, for there was so much to be told. First of all, Mrs. Pringle told mamma that the government had ordered that all property belonging to Mrs. Allston, the sister of James L. Petigru, should be protected from all damage. This seemed to impress Mrs. Pringle very much, but mamma did not seem to attach much importance to it. She said she did not think it was at all to be depended on, that she must go to Georgetown and get the commanding officer there to send a detachment of men to take from the negroes the keys of the barns at each plantation, where the large crops made were locked up. These keys they had given to the negroes, and mamma could get no corn for the horses nor provisions for herself, and they must restore the keys to her. Mrs. Pringle said it would be quite useless for her to ask anything until she took the oath of allegiance to the United States, that she had wanted something done and their reply was until she took the oath of allegiance no request could be considered; that she had declined to do so at the time, but now felt it must be done. So it was arranged that mamma would take Mrs. Pringle down in her carriage to Georgetown the next day to take the oath, while I should remain with Mary and her brothers at the White House.

Oh, what a white day that stands out in my memory! I was embroidering a waist in black silk, to make a Russian blouse out of the everlasting purple calico we were all wearing. As I sewed in a big chair in the beautiful library, filled with most delightful books, exquisite engravings on the walls and marble busts around the room, Mr. Pringle read aloud to me. He picked up the first book his hand came upon, — I think it was "Eugene Aram." But the book was nothing; it was his voice, so beautifully modulated, and his presence, safe back from the awful danger, and in his own beautiful home. It cast a spell over me; and long afterward he told me he had no idea of what he was reading; nothing of it entered his mind; it was the simple fact of having me sitting there in his own home, sewing as if I belonged there, that intoxicated him, so that he was afraid to speak, and so took refuge in reading! So there we were, a pair of idiots, in a fool's paradise, some might think, but such moments are immortal. Soul speaks to soul, though no voice be heard.

CHAPTER XXVI

TAKING THE OATH

THAT evening reality returned heavily when the two mothers, widows and managers of large estates and property, returned. The day had been very trying. The oath was taken as the first thing, they having made up their minds to take it at once. Then mamma asked the colonel to send a guard or a single soldier to take back the keys which they had given to the negroes and give them to her, the rightful owner of the foodstuffs in the barns. He said quite nonchalantly that she could take the keys; it was not at all necessary for him to send a guard; he would give her a written order. She remonstrated with him, saying she believed in authority, and as an officer had delivered the key to the negroes, taking it from the overseer, a white man who was in charge of the plantation, she thought it was absolutely necessary that an official or a man wearing the United States uniform should take the keys from the negroes and deliver them to her; that, without that, there was an opening for dispute and contention and disrespect. The colonel said shortly he did not agree with her. She then asked about the order from Washington as to the protection of her property. Yes, he said that he had received such an order, but they knew of nothing to which it would apply. He wrote an order for the negroes to deliver the keys to her, and the interview was ended. She had some business of a different nature which she attended to in Georgetown, and then they drove back to the White House, very tired and very indignant at the want of courtesy, and desire to facilitate the return of things to a possible working order. The negroes were free — no one had a word to say on that score — but they were not owners of the land, and in order for things to assume a condition when the land could be planted, or, rather, prepared for planting, in the new order of things, the negroes would look to the officers for the tone they were expected to assume to their former owners. But it was evident these men absolutely refused to back up the white people in any way. The talk that evening was not cheering, to say the least.

Mrs. Pringle told us, after the Georgetown matter had been fully discussed, of her experience with the man, Bunker, who had led the negroes to Plantersville and behaved so outrageously there, after turning over all the houses on the river, Chicora Wood included, to the negroes, to distribute all the contents among themselves. It was two days afterward that he came down to the White House, followed by an immense throng of negroes, and demanded wine and money. Mrs. Pringle, who was as bold as a lion and very clever, tall, stout, and of commanding presence, with the face of a man, met them on the piazza and refused to let them enter the house. Bunker had been drinking heavily and also some of the negroes. She spoke with authority, and said she knew the United States Government would not sanction the seizure of her things by a drunken mob, even though one man, the leader, had on the United States uniform; and the army regulations were severe against intoxication. She was a Northern woman herself and knew all about it, and had friends in the government and the army at that moment. Bunker was a little dashed, but very angry at being talked to in that haughty manner before his followers, and things looked ugly for a moment, so that Mary, who was standing behind her mother, began to cry, and, Bunker's attention being diverted to her, he began to try to console her. She was a very beautiful girl. He brought forward some of the things he had stolen from the Plantersville people and presented them to her — silver pitchers, etc. Mary indignantly pushed them away, but her mother bent down and said: "Take them; you can restore them to the owner." So Mary let him bring them into the piazza and present them to her, but when he began to try to console her by complimentary speeches and admiring looks, she dropped her full length on the piazza in a dead faint! Mrs. Pringle took her by the feet and dragged her in through the hall to the dining-room, and, locking the door, put the key in her pocket, and returned to the mob; but they had vanished away, leaving rapidly and quietly. They, no doubt, thought Mary was dead; those kind of people do not faint, and to see her brilliant, radiant color suddenly turn to deadly white and her mother drag her limp body away like that sobered them. In the meantime the man whom they trusted as house-servant had busied himself getting out — the keys being in the basket in the drawing-room — all the wine and liquor there was in the house. He packed it up, and took it out of the back door to a cart which he had there, and went off with the party. He was never seen by them again. When they had all gone, Mrs.

Pringle unlocked the door, and used restoratives, and finally succeeded in bringing Mary to life, but she was terribly weak and ill for some days. Mrs. Pringle reviled Mary for being such a weakling and failing her at a critical moment, but we all felt and she knew that Mary had really saved the day, diverting the unsteady mind of Bunker from his original intention of plunder, first her tears and then her faint had converted his rage first to pity and then to fright.

The next morning mamma and I left the hospitable, beautiful White House after breakfast and drove to Nightingale Hall, about two miles away. Here the negroes had been specially turbulent. The overseer there, Mr. Sweat, was a very good, quiet man, and had been liked by all the negroes, but in the intoxication of freedom their first exercise of it was to tell Mr. Sweat if he left the house they would kill him, and they put a negro armed with a shotgun to guard the house and see that he did not leave alive. Mr. Sweat seems to have been something of a philosopher, for he assured them he had no intention of leaving, and settled himself quite cheerfully to pass the time of his imprisonment. The key of the barns having been given to the negroes, he kept a little journal of all they did. From his window he watched them take supplies from the barns, corn and rice, using the baskets which were always used in measuring grain, open baskets made to hold a bushel, which is thirty-two quarts. In this way, as he knew exactly what was in the barns, having superintended the planting, harvesting, and threshing of the grains, he could tell just how much was left. He had written all of this to my mother, getting a friendly negro who cooked for him to take charge of the letter.

When we drove in the yard the negroes soon assembled in great numbers. Mamma had not seen them at all yet. She talked with the foreman, Mack, very pleasantly from the seat in the carriage, asking after all the old people on the place, and his family, etc. Then, finally, she said:

"And now, Mack, I want the keys to the barn."

He said: "De officer giv me de key, ma'am, en I kyant gie um to yu."

She drew from her silk reticule the order, and said: "I have here the officer's order to you to give the key to me."

He took the paper and looked at it, but there rose a sullen murmur from the crowd, and a young man who had stood a little way off, balancing a sharp stone in his hand and aiming it at mamma from time to time, now came nearer and leaned on the wheel of the carriage. Mamma thought he wanted to intimidate her, and so she stepped out of the carriage into the very midst of them. I motioned to follow, but she said in a low tone, as she shut the door, "Stay where you are," and I obeyed.

The foreman said: "How we gwine eat ef we gie yu de key? We haf fu hab bittle."

Mamma answered: "Mack, you know that every man, woman, and child on this place has full ration for a year! You know, for you measured it and gave it out yourself. If anything should be wanted, I will come down and give it out my-self."

At that the young man, still balancing the stone, laughed, and all followed in a great shout, and he said: "Yu kyant do dat, dat de man wuk. Yu kyan do um, en we'll starve."

But mamma held her ground, and walking up and down among them, speaking to each one by name, asking after their children and babies, all by name. Gradually the tension relaxed, and after a long time, it seemed to me ages, in which she showed no irritation, no impatience, only friendly interest, no sense that they could possibly be enemies, Mack gave her the keys without any interference from the others, and we left. She did not think it wise to go to the barn to look at the crops. Having gained her point, she thought it best to leave. We were both terribly exhausted when we got home, and enjoyed a good night's rest in our own very original-looking log house in Plantersville, which Charley had succeeded in getting made clean and comfortable for us.

The next morning, after breakfast, we started to Chicora Wood to get the keys there. Mamma did not take Charley, for he was very weak from his illness, and having made the trip down before he was strong enough. Besides that, in the condition of the country, the negroes were apt to be more irritated by the presence of a returned soldier than with ladies only. Besides which, it was a very mortifying position for a man, whose impulse, under insolence or refusal to do the right thing, was naturally to resent it, and, being perfectly powerless, not having taken the oath, he was not even recognized as a citizen, and had no rights and would have no support from the law. Therefore, it was certainly the part of wisdom to

[267]

leave him behind, though I did not fully understand it at the time. We did not have much trouble at Chicora. Daddy Primus had been the man to whom the keys were given, and he was a very superior, good old man. He had been head carpenter ever since Daddy Thomas's death. He took mamma into each barn and showed her the splendid crops, and as he locked the door to each, she just held out her hand for it, and he placed the key to that barn in her hands without question. And here the people seemed glad to see her and to see me, and we walked about over the place and talked with every one.

We looked at the house; it was a wreck, — the front steps gone, not a door nor shutter left, and not a sash. They had torn out all the mahogany framework around the doors and windows — there were mahogany panels below the windows and above the doors there were panels painted — the mahogany banisters to the staircase going upstairs; everything that could be torn away was gone. The pantry steps being there, we went into the house, went all through, even into the attic. Then the big tank for the supply of the water-works, which was lined with zinc, had been torn to pieces, and the bathroom below entirely torn up. It was a scene of destruction, and papa's study, where he kept all his accounts and papers, as he had done from the time he began planting as a young man, was almost waist-deep in torn letters and papers. Poor things, they were looking, I suppose, for money or treasure of some kind in all those bundles of letters and papers most methodically and carefully tied up with red tape, each packet of accounts having a wooden slat, with the date and subject of account upon it. We looked through every corner, and then went out on the piazza and sat down and ate the lunch we had brought. It is wonderful to me, as I look back, that we were so cheerful; but we were, and after a good lunch with some hard-boiled eggs Maum Mary brought us, we got into the carriage and drove home to the dear, peaceful log house.

The next morning we started early in the carriage for Guendalos, mamma and I, driven by Daddy Aleck. This plantation belonged to my elder brother, Colonel Ben Allston, who had been in the army since the beginning of the war, never having been home at all. There had been no white man on the place, and we heard the negroes were most turbulent and excited. As we neared the place the road was lined on either side by angry, sullen black faces; instead of the pleasant smile and courtesy or bow to which we were accustomed, not a sign of recognition or welcome, only an ominous silence. As the carriage passed on they formed an irregular line and followed.

This would be a test case, as it were. If the keys were given up, it would mean that the former owners still had some rights. We drove into the barnyard and stopped in front of the barn. Several hundred negroes were there, and as they had done the day before, they crowded closer and closer around the carriage, and mamma got out into the midst of them, as she had done at Nightingale. She called for the head man and told him she wished to see the crop, and he cleared the way before us to the rice barn and then to the corn barn. Mamma complimented him on the crops. As she was about to leave the corn barn a woman stretched her arms across the wide door so as to hold up the passageway. Mamma said, "Sukey, let me pass," but Sukey did not budge. Then mamma turned to Jacob. "This woman has lost her hearing; you must make her move from the doorway." Very gently Jacob pushed her aside and we went out and Jacob locked the door.

Then mamma said: "And now, Jacob, I want the keys." "No, ma'am, I kyant gie yu de key. De officer gen me de key, en I kyant gie um to nobody but de officer."

"I have the officer's written order to you to give me the keys — here it is" — and she drew from her reticule the paper and handed it to Jacob. He examined it carefully and returned it to her, and proceeded slowly to draw the keys from his pocket and was about to hand them to mamma, when a young man who had stood near, with a threatening expression sprang forward and shouted, "Ef yu gie up de key, blood'll flow," shaking his fist at Jacob. Then the crowd took up the shout, "Yes, blood'll flow for true," and a deafening clamor followed. Jacob returned the keys to the depths of his pocket. The crowd, yelling, talking, gesticulating, pressed closer and closer upon us, until there was scarcely room to stand. Daddy Aleck had followed with the carriage as closely as the crowd would allow without trampling some one, and now said to mamma: "Miss, yu better git een de carriage." Mamma answered by saying: "Aleck, go and bring Mas' Charles here."

Most reluctantly the old man obeyed, and drove

off, leaving us alone in the midst of this raging crowd. I must say my heart sank as I saw the carriage with the faithful old man disappear down the avenue — for there was no white person within five miles and in this crowd there was certainly not one friendly negro. Jacob, the head man, was the most so, but evidently he was in great fear of the others and incapable of showing his good feeling openly. I knew that Daddy Aleck would have to drive five miles to find Charley and then back, and that must consume a great deal of time.

The crowd continued to clamor and yell, first one thing and then another, but the predominant cry was: "Go for de officer — fetch de Yankee." Mamma said: "By all means bring the officer; I wish to see him quite as much as you do."

The much-desired and talked-of officer was fourteen miles away. In the midst of the uproar a new man came running and shouting out that the officers were at a plantation three miles away, so six men started at a run to fetch him. Mamma and I walked slowly down the avenue to the public road, with a yelling mob of men, women, and children around us. They sang sometimes in unison, sometimes in parts, strange words which we did not understand, followed by a much-repeated chorus:

"I free, I free!
I free as a frog!
I free till I fool!
Glory Alleluia!"

They revolved around us, holding out their skirts and dancing — now with slow, swinging movements, now with rapid jig-motions, but always with weird chant and wild gestures. When the men sent for the officer reached the gate they turned and shouted, "Don't let no white man een dat gate," which was answered by many voices, "No, no, we won't let no white pusson een, we'll chop um down wid hoe — we'll chop um to pieces sho" — and they brandished their large, sharp, gleaming rice-field hoes, which looked most formidable weapons truly. Those who had not hoes were armed with pitchforks and hickory sticks, and some had guns.

It was a strange situation: Two women, one fifty, the other eighteen, pacing up and down the road between two dense hedges of angry blacks, while a little way off in the woods was a company of men, drawn up in something like military order — guns held behind them — solemn, silent, gloomy, a contrast to the noisy mob around us.

[273]

There we paced for hours while the autumn day wore on.

In the afternoon Daddy Aleck returned without Charley, having failed to find him. It was a great relief to me, for though I have been often laughed at for the opinion, I hold that there is a certain kind of chivalry in the negroes — they wanted blood, they wanted to kill some one, but they couldn't make up their minds to kill two defenseless ladies; but if Charley had been found and brought, I firmly believe it would have kindled the flame. When the carriage came, I said to mamma in a low tone: "Let us go now."

She answered with emphasis, but equally low, "Say not one word about going; we must stay until the officers come" — so we paced on, listening to blasphemous mutterings and threats, but appearing not to hear at all — for we talked together as we walked about the autumn flowers and red berries, and the brilliant skies, just as though we had been on our own piazza. I heard the little children say to each other: "Luk a dem buckra 'oman, ain't 'fraid."

The sun sank in a blaze of glory, and I began to wonder if we would spend the night there, when there was a cry, "Dey comin'!" We thought it was the officers, and how I did wish they could come and see us there, but it turned out to be four of the runners, who had returned, saying they had not found the officers, and that Jacob and one of the men had gone on to Georgetown to see them. Then we got into the carriage and drove home. We were hungry and exhausted, having tasted no morsel of food or drop of water through the long day. We went to bed in our log castle, which had no lock of any kind on the door, and slept soundly.

In the early dawn of the next morning there was a knock at the door, and before we could reach the hallway the door was opened, and a black hand thrust through, with the keys. No word was spoken — it was Jacob; he gave them in silence, and mamma received them with the same solemnity.

The bloodless battle had been won.

CHARLES PETIGRU ALLSTON'S NARRATIVE

During the war there was great demand for horses, which increased as the time went on. My father always raised a few horses, and at this time there was a gray stallion (part Arab), just four years old, that my father had given to me the winter before he died; there were also several other horses, saddle and draft. After my father's death, my mother, in the summer of 1864, made an arrangement with some friends in the Cavalry Service, C. S. A., Butler's Command, to take and use our horses, with the promise that any that survived should be returned to us after the war.

One of the horses was killed under Edward L. Wells, of the Charleston Light Dragoons, as Butler's Scouts were leaving Cheraw, S. C., by a Parrot shell that passed through him, going in at the tail and coming out of the chest, did not explode, and left Wells uninjured.

My gray stallion was ridden by Julius Pringle all through Virginia, wherever Butler's Cavalry went, and returned safe and sound. The other two horses, a gray gelding and a bay filly, were alive at the time of the surrender, and Julius Pringle turned them over to a young negro of ours, who had been sent along with the horses, in charge of them (Sam Galant) somewhere in Virginia, and told him to make his way back home, and to get away before the actual surrender. The lad was of a family who had been long in our service, family servants for generations; his father had been my father's body-servant for years, and then been succeeded in that office by one of his sons, and Sam had grown up with me. My father had sent him to Charleston to be instructed in music by Mr. Dauer, a German, with three others, and he played the violin very well. This boy had no money that we knew of, food was scarce, straggling marauders many, the horses in pretty poor shape, yet he managed to work his way with two horses through the country, and arrive at Crowley Hill safe, but nearly starved, both he and the horses, specially the gray. I asked him afterward how he managed it; he said he seldom moved during the day, but got out of the way as much as possible, and let the horses eat grass; then at night he travelled, but was careful to avoid all other travellers, and also all camp-fires. He must have done some very adroit foraging, also, or he would surely have starved. Horses were specially valuable then, and we were glad to see these two return.

After things settled down somewhat, in May, 1865, I think, my mother decided that she would have to go to the plantation home in Georgetown County to look after affairs there, and try to restore order. A deserter from the fleet off the coast had gone through all the plantations near

Georgetown, and incited the negroes to plunder and rob in every direction, and had caused much trouble and demoralization. Several fine dwellings had been completely destroyed, and all of them robbed of every movable article. My mother and one of my sisters started in the carriage, with a pair of horses driven by old Aleck — I rode along on horseback — Julius Pringle, also on horseback, joined us. There was practically no law in the land, but the influence of established authority in the past kept a very fair semblance of order. We had a journey of over ninety miles ahead of us, roads and everything uncertain, but we made the trip safely and with little incident, and arrived safely at Plantersville, which was a collection of houses built irregularly in the pineland, as summer homes for the rice-planters along the rivers, who had to leave the comfortable plantation homes in May and go to the rough pineland houses until November, on account of malaria fever. Our summer house was on the sea, and could not be occupied at all during the war, so my father had built by his carpenters in this settlement a large log house, on lightwood pillars ten feet high, to escape damp, and put on it a double roof of cypress shingles, in which there was not a single metal nail; they were securely fastened on with wooden pins. (Up to the year 1900 this roof did not have to be renewed.) To this log house my mother, sister, and myself were to go.

.   .   .   .

After a while we had to set to work to gather in some of the furniture which the negroes had carried off and hidden, for we had not enough to get along with; my mother, having taken the oath as soon as she returned to the low country, some time before, applied to the military authorities, and a corporal and three men were detailed to assist in recovering what we could find. . . . There were some wild and weird scenes enacted. The nigs had been told that everything would belong to them; that the government would punish the whites for the war, by taking their property and dividing it among the nigs, giving forty acres to each head of family, etc. So when we arrived, backed by soldiers, to take from them what they had collected of our belongings, they were much taken aback, and some of them were inclined to resist. However, we gathered up enough furniture and stuff to get along comfortably.

.   .   .   .

Then came the agreements as to planting; what portion of the crop they should have in payment of their labor, and what portion we, the owners of the land, should have; here again the military had to be called in. One lieutenant, who was trying to argue with a violent gang, finally turned to my mother and said, with a most troubled face: "Mrs. Allston, I think I would rather have white help." He could do nothing with them, and a man of sterner mould had to come another day and make the contract with that gang.

But in Plantersville we young folk took every opportunity possible to have a dance or some frolic at night. It was certainly most wholesome to have some diversion from the serious problems of the day.

PART V

READJUSTMENT

CHAPTER XXVII

GLEAMS OF LIGHT FROM MY DIARY

Log Castle, Plantersville, July 10th, 1865.

IT seems too wonderful to be at home again in my own dear low country after being refugees so long. It is a delight to be alive, and know most of those we love are alive too after the terrible sufferings and anxieties of the War. We miss Papa more and more every day; it seems impossible it should be only a year and three months since he died, it seems years and years. Poor Mamma, who was perfectly unaccustomed to business, has had every thing upon her, and it is a perfect wonder to see her rise to each emergency as it comes. Yesterday she called Daddy Aleck and told him she had not the money to pay his wages and he would have to find another place.

He was very indignant. "Miss, I don' want no wagis! Aint I wuk fu yu sence I bin man grown, aint my fadder wuk fu Maussa fadder! En my grandfadder de same! Aint yu feed me on de bes'! An' clothes me in de bes'. Aint I drive yo', de Guvna's lady all de time Maussa bin

[283]

Guv'na, en now yu tink I gwine lef' yu, en lef' de hosses. 'Tis true I got but a po' pair, jes' wat dem Yankee lef', but I kin manige wid dem, en I wont lef' dem en yu to dat triflin niggah boy, no ma'am, not Aleck Pa'ka, e aint mean enuf fu dat!"

It was a distressing scene. Mamma was much moved, but she was firm, and when Daddy Aleck realized that she would not be persuaded, the tears rolled down his shiny black face and I, in my corner pretending to write, ignominiously sobbed. When Daddy Aleck had gone, I remonstrated with Mamma. I did not see how we could get on without the old man, and he did not want to go, he would be content to stay if he had his food and clothes as usual, and I thought it was cruel.

Mamma said, "Child, you don't understand; Aleck really wants to stay now, but I have no right to keep him. He is a valuable groom and hostler, can manage and drive any horses, and he can easily get a good place in Georgetown, whereas I could not only not pay him, but I could not possibly feed him as he has been accustomed to be fed, sugar and coffee and tea and all the meat he wanted. We barely have what will keep the household, and a very little coffee and tea. As to clothing him, that means a heavy outlay and is out of the question."

As I still argued, she said, "My dear Bessie, why make things harder for me? Try and trust to my desire to do the best I can under great trial and strain." Of course, I was ashamed of myself, and tried to say so; but I am a stubborn brute and find it hard to say I'm sorry even when I am.

Aug. 1st. My days are so happy. I cut and contrive new garments out of old, and sew and dream as I sew. Brother's wife, Ellen, is very pretty and very sweet, but very ill, it seems to me. She cannot walk or do anything but lie still and read and talk; this last she is always ready to do, and while I rub her, as I do twice a day to try and give some strength to her limbs, she talks most entertainingly. She has been a great belle and was engaged to three other men when she married Brother. She was surprised when she first told me and I appeared shocked. It seems, in Texas, it is thought nothing of, but I solemnly advised her not to mention it here, at which she laughed heartily. Afterwards, I could not help laughing myself, for Brother has had rather a varied career in the way of engagements, but I did not tell her this.

[285]

I have been crazy to have some low necked waists to wear in the late afternoon and evenings. I always used to dress for the evenings, and I am so tired of these everlasting calico frocks which we are all wearing. Papa was lucky enough to get a piece of purple calico two years ago, which ran the Blockade. We were enchanted, it was rather a pretty pattern, purple stripes on a white ground and a little flower in each stripe. We were much in need of frocks so Mamma had made for us each two dresses and she had two herself. From that day we have been in uniform. I cut my waist myself so as to have it different. I made a Russian blouse and embroidered the shoulder straps and sleeves and belt in black, but, alas, the difference is only waist deep. The rest is just like the other eight! Two weeks ago I had a brilliant idea. Della's bedroom curtains were pink and white chintz and were lined with pink paper cambric. The sun has faded the linings hopelessly into every shade of yellow and brown, in some places almost white. That gave me the thought that if I bleached those linings, I might have some white material to make into waists, so I went to the plantation and consulted Maum Milly. She looked at the stuff and thought it could be done. Told me how to wash it first, then let it lie in cold water a day or so, then spread it on the grass and leave it for the sun and dew to bleach, and she thought, in two or three weeks, it would be white. She has always been our laundress, but now of course we cannot pay her and have just a little girl her granddaughter doing the washing. After having given me all the directions of what to tell the "gal" to do, I said I would not think of trusting it to Clarissa. I was going to do it myself. Then Maum Milly's heart relented and she said, "Chile, yu kyant do um proper. Gim me dat cloth, I'll do um fu yu." So now I know if it can be done, it will be.

Aug. 10*th*. Maum Milly brought my white stuff, looking like a fine piece of muslin, and I have made two lovely low necked baby waists. They are too sweet, gathered very full and little short sleeves also gathered full, and around the neck and sleeves I have put the beautiful valenciennes lace Mamma gave me, and they are things of beauty. No one would ever dream they were evolved from faded pink paper cambric curtain linings. Mrs. Pringle and Mary, who are very critical, having lived much in the great world, admired my waist very much last night when they had a little dance at their house. I was careful not to tell its history.

They are such an addition to this little village for, though in deep grief for the loss of Poinsett who was killed at Haw's Ship, Mrs. Pringle is so thankful to have her other two sons alive and with her that, though he was the darling of her heart, she keeps herself and her house as cheerful as possible, and does all she can to make the village brighter. Most people think it proper to be very gloomy. Of course, it is hard, all the people who were rich are now very poor but there is no good being gloomy over it. So Mrs. Pringle gives little dances now and then, and they are delightful. Then we have riding parties. Dear old Daddy Aleck saved two of our side saddles for us. I am so glad mine was one.

Thanks to Sam for bringing home the horse and Daddy Aleck for the saddle, I am able to ride; and, as every body is afraid of tête-a-têtes, we go in parties, four girls and four men, all riding together. I say afraid of tête-a-têtes because the War is still so very near, and it is hard to keep to surface talk, and it is awfully dangerous to go below, for we are all paupers.

Mamma has gone to Charleston to see if she can

arrange to have our house repaired. Three shells went through the roof and it is impossible to live in it until it is thoroughly repaired. I do hope she will succeed, but she has not a cent of money, and nowhere to borrow any. It does seem desperate, but I must remember when Papa was dying and Mamma in despair said, "What shall we do without you?" He answered steadily, in spite of his gasping breath, "The Lord will provide." And we have been marvellously helped and guided.

Aug. 25th. A letter from Mamma today has upset me completely. She has been very successful in getting the house repaired. A contractor who knew her well and had worked for Papa and done up the house the last time, undertook to do all the work without any payment now; but, when he has finished, Mamma will give him her note promising to pay as soon as she can. This has lifted a great load, but the tremendous announcement is that she has determined to open a boarding and day school, and she expects me *to teach!* The minute I read the letter I wrote, "Mamma, I cannot teach. Don't ask me to do it. I just hate the thought. Besides, I don't know enough of any one thing to teach it. I cannot, indeed, I cannot." Now that I have sent the letter I am

[289]

awfully ashamed, and when we were riding this afternoon, we fell a little behind the others and I told Mr. P. He seemed so shocked and surprised. Altogether I am miserable. Am I really just a butterfly? Is my love of pleasure the strongest thing about me? What an awful thought. I try to pray, but I don't want to pray. I just do want to be for a while like a flower in the sun. I want to open and feel the glow and the beauty and the joy of existing, even if I know I have to wither and die sometime. Flowers don't think of that, they just rejoice in the life God has made so beautiful for them, and I do believe He likes that. Oh dear, how I wish I was good or dead, one or the other. Now I must go and rub my pretty sweet sister-in-law, and try to forget how wicked I am.

Sept. 1st. A letter from Mamma in answer to my protest that I could not teach. "My dear Bessie, your letter was a great surprise. It would be a serious disappointment if all the money your Father so gladly spent on your education has been wasted. However, I think you do yourself an injustice. At any rate, you will come down for the opening of the school and we will see."

That is all, no reproaches for my petulance and

miserable selfishness. But I notice she does not confide her plans to me any more, and that hurts more than bitter words. "Oh, wretched man that I am, who shall deliver me from the body of this Death." I don't believe I have quoted it right, but that means *self*. Mr. Glennie in our Bible lesson once told us that in some Eastern country the punishment for a murderer was to bind the body of his victim with chains on his back, and he must wander ever with this putrifying result of his crime, until it crumbled away. What an awful punishment, and how suitable. Mr. Glennie did not tell us it meant one's own wretched self in that cry, but I know it does by my own experience. One is never free from that burden self. Happy those, I suppose, in whom it perishes by disintegration before they get old. Alas, alas, in some it seems well nigh indestructible !

Sept. 3rd. We cannot have any service in the dear little old log church, for Mr. Trapier will not pray for the President of the United States, and so we have not the pleasure and comfort of church.

Mr. P. comes every day and reads aloud to me. It is really unique. I sit inside the window and sew on my ingenious remakings of old things and he sits outside the window and reads, "He knew He was Right." It is perfectly delightful for me, it is so much easier than talking. People are so disagreeable, the village is all saying we are engaged. I know he is hearing it all the time, as I am, and it is so awkward for both. I thought it would be easier if I referred lightly to it, so this morning, sewing very fast, pricking my first finger brutally, I said, "Last evening I was walking in the village and heard something so absurdly ridiculous." I got no farther, for in a solemn, hurt voice, from across the window sill, there came, "I'm sorry it seemed so ridiculous to you. It did not seem so to me." Then I took refuge in immoderate laughter, after which I said, "Please go on with the book." But I felt I had been defeated in my effort to make things more comfortable.

Sept. 15*th.* The wild flowers are so beautiful all through the woods. I do not walk in the village now, people are so trying. I go out into the swamp behind the house every afternoon. There are great tiger lilies and the gorgeous Cardinal Flower, I call it scarlet lobelia. In the up country where we have been for four years, I never saw these flowers. Then the ferns and the lovely little partridge berry vine. This is called the lover's vine sometimes, because there are two lovely sweet little white flowers, with the delicate perfume of the orange blossom, and when they drop there is formed only one scarlet berry, but it has two little eyes. It grows along the ground. Its dark green, regularly placed leaves and bright berries are too pretty. I mean to take some up and plant it in a box to take to Charleston with me, to remind me of this dear darling country.

Riding two afternoons ago, we were galloping along four abreast, as if for a charge, when Dot shied from a snake alongside the road, and my saddle turned completely under her, and I found myself under my neighbour's horse! He was so frightened and so was every one else that they all seemed indignant at my laughing. It seemed unsuitable to the situation, but it really was too funny, I seated in the middle of the road under Mr. P.'s horse, whose name is Trovatore and who behaved beautifully and did not trample me or hurt me at all. Everyone was pale and clamorous for restoratives, which I did not in the least need. My saddle was put back and secured and we had a very silent ride home in spite of my efforts to talk.

Sept. 26th. Every one said my delightful soli-

tary strolls in the swamp would end in fever, and
every one is happy now for they were right and I
have been laid low for a week. As there was no
one here to take care of me, Ellen requiring great
care herself, Mrs. Pringle, who adds to her other
great qualities that of being a competent nurse,
has been coming over every day to take care of
me. It is delightful, for she is so clever and (for
the moment) so sympathetic that I positively enjoy the state of things except when I am actually
burning up with fever. Dr. Dan Tucker is attending me, and is a delightful Doctor. I was
burning up with thirst, my fever so high and the
practice of the country is to give water by the
teaspoonful in fever. To my delight and the surprise of the inhabitants, especially that revered personage, the oldest, the Doctor, ordered a pail of
water brought fresh from the spring and put by
my bedside with a dear little gourd dipper, and
told me to drink all I wanted! It was so clever
of him, for it is so much to satisfy the eye and the
imagination. I really do not drink so much, but
I feel refreshed and satisfied by its presence and
the fact that I can have all I want. I am sitting
up today and so bored by the absence of Mrs.

Pringle that I have to write to pass the time. Dr. Dan Tucker was educated in Paris, that is, took his medical course there. He served through the War as Surgeon and has now settled here.

Sept. 28th. Dr. Tucker wants me fed up, and Mrs. Pringle is bringing me over delicious things to eat, made by herself for she is a distinguished cook. The Doctor shot and sent me a most beautiful summer duck two days ago. I enjoyed some of it very much, but the next day came out in huge splotches of red all over me. Mrs. Pringle was quite scared, but the Doctor said that the food was a little too strong for me yet awhile, and I must have no more till I was able to walk about.

Oct. 13th. Wild excitement! Letter from Mamma, Della has a little daughter! I am an Aunt! As if that was not excitement enough, Mamma writes I must go down to Charleston at once. The house is not yet ready, but Aunt Petigru has invited me to stay there until we are able to move into the house. I am pleased and yet I am sorry. I hate to have this summer, the happiest of my life, end. And yet I knew it had to end, and it was time. I have let myself just dream and dream, and, when one has to work, it is not good to dream.

I have been far from idle in body; I have kept the house, and nursed Ellen, and rubbed her, kneeling morning and evening for an hour at a time by the bed and not minding my own back aching till I nearly drop, and I have sewed and done many other necessary things, but all the time I have been dreaming, and I do love it. But now I must be stern and say, "Get behind me, Satan," when the dreaminess wants to seize me. The bell is ringing, I must go.

Oct. 20th. The last few days have been trying. I have had so much trouble to keep on the surface. I am going tomorrow. Brother will drive me to Georgetown to take the boat. My irresponsible life ends. It has not lasted long, for, Brother being away, I had all the copying of Papa's will to send to the different members of the family, and the lists of the negroes and the plantations and all the property to make, and it is only these two months, since Brother has been at home and has taken charge of everything, that I have been able to enjoy being young and foolish. I love dancing and I love admiration and I love to be gay; but all the time, underneath all that, I am so terribly serious, so terribly in earnest that

[296]

I find the other girls do not understand me and the men are startled and puzzled — all but my friend, and I have to be so fiercely foolish and on the surface with him if I am to prevent a catastrophe, and I must prevent it.

CHAPTER XXVIII

AUNT PETIGRU — MY FIRST GERMAN

Charleston, Oct. 25th.

MY niece is too fascinating, tiny, red, squirming! I have never been on intimate terms with so young a baby before, and cannot be content to hold her but a little while. I want to hold her for a long time and realize her individuality, but the nurse disapproves, so I continue to find her fascinating.

Oct. 30th. I am having a delightful time. Aunt is very good and kind. She is the widow of Mamma's brother, James L. Petigru, who was a distinguished lawyer and codified the Laws of this State. He died in the midst of the War, heartbroken, they said, at the suffering and distress for his own people that he saw ahead. Poor Mamma, it was awfully hard on her, for she simply adored Uncle, and Papa was as strongly in favour of secession as Uncle was opposed to it. So those she loved best were absolutely opposed to each other. Her opinions went with Papa, but she felt intense sympathy for Uncle, and felt it killed him. The Yankee Officers have been ordered by the Government to treat Aunt with the greatest consideration. She has but to signify a wish for it to be gratified at once. She was a great beauty and has never forgotten it through years of terrible ill health. Uncle spoiled and humoured her always, and now it seems the most natural thing in the world to have everything she wants, have officers at her beck and call and live in luxury, when every one else is almost in want. But she is most generous with her comforts and luxuries, having Nannie, her maid and nurse, seek out her friends who are ill or in need and sending them baskets from her stores. She does not hesitate to say that she did not in any way sympathize with Uncle's opinion as to the War. She is always in bed, and with a much befrilled cap which only reveals a few curls of light yellow hair, receives the officers sent to her for command. She has a very small single bed quite low to the floor and looks like a child, and speaks in a high childish voice, most authoritatively. She has what she calls a "Lazy Scissors." It shoots out to a length of about three feet and picks up things she wants. Nannie, her black maid, rules everything and everybody, and I am thankful Nannie happens to approve of me for it helps the situation. Aunt has a critical eye and loves beauty, and I am not pretty, but she also loves to laugh, and I can amuse her by my accounts of all my adventures when I go out, for I never stir from the house without some adventure. Just now I am trying to get Aunt to consent to my going to a party which is to be given by the young men at Miss Annie Savage Heyward's house, corner of Lamboll and Legare. It is the first big dance given in town and I want to go, but Aunt has not as yet given her consent. Mamma has gone in the country for a while and there is no appeal from Aunt's decision. I have got Nannie on my side. The trouble is there is no chaperone to go with me, only my Cousin Charley Porcher will come for me and bring me home. He fought all through the War and came out alive, and I'm sure that makes him fit for anything.

Nov. 5th. Well, I went to the party and had a grand time, no refreshments but water, but a beautifully waxed floor, a great big cool room, that is, two opening into each other with folding doors, and a great wide piazza all round outside to walk in after dancing. But first I must tell about my getting off. There had been no question of dress, I was thankful for that. Aunt

[300]

seemed to think of course I had a ball dress. So
when I was arrayed in my best black merino skirt
— I was still in half mourning for Papa — and my
bleached pink paper cambric baby waist, and Aunt
sent Nannie to say she wished to see me before I
went, I trembled. However, I summoned up all
the diablerie in me to meet the ordeal. Really, I
felt most uncertain of my appearance already, but
I would not show it for worlds. When I went in
to the darkened room, Aunt ordered Nannie to
light up everything, candles and lamps, and as I
stood trembling inside, while the lights asserted
themselves, Aunt surveyed me and burst forth.

"Bessie, you are a fool! My God, that is no
costume for a party! You look more like a funeral
than a big fashionable dance! Come here and let
me see that skirt. My God, it is really what I
thought, black merino! Plain and full! You
cannot leave my house for a party dressed like
that!"

"Aunt," I said, "If you say another word I will
begin to cry and then my costume will be lighted
up with a red nose to please you." This made her
laugh and I went on. "You have not looked at
the exquisite lace on my bodice. Mrs. Pringle said
this was an ideal young girl's waist."

She looked, examined the lace, and relented. "Nannie, open that top drawer to the left and get out that set of old Mexican silver. This child must have something to relieve this stern effect."

Nannie arrived with a box and Aunt took out and had me put on a pair of broad silver bracelets like manacles of fish scales, a string of silver beads round my neck which though not plump is called pretty, and in my ears carved silver earrings about three inches long and weighing about a ton apiece. Then Aunt surveyed me once more, gave me a little push and said, "Now go, all this excitement has made me feel very ill. Do behave yourself and don't cry if you don't get a partner."

Thankfully I escaped and went down to Charley, who was tired waiting for me. He was all admiration of my appearance, but Aunt had injected a new and fearful thought to my mind. "Not get a partner," what an awful thought! I had always had my choice of partners, but now that I came to think, I had been away from town all the years of the War. Papa and Mamma had never allowed me to accept invitations to stay with my friends who had remained in Charleston. It was said that society was too informal and too gay for them to be willing for me to join it. Most of the dear boy friends whom I used to dance with had been killed or disabled, and I really was going into an unknown company. I suppose it was well that Aunt's words had made me realize this, for it might have come with too great a shock without that. As we went in, Charley gave me my only pair of well worn slippers which he had carried, and I went into the dressing room and, taking off my walking boots, (an awful pair of English shoes, miles too big for me and stuffed with cotton, which I had worn for two years, we having been lucky to get them through the blockade), put them on. Then I braced myself up and went upstairs with Charley. Miss Annie Heyward received us and put me at my ease at once by asking if I could play a galop, for none of the girls who could play had arrived yet, and so she had to ask me etc., etc. I was delighted and went with alacrity to the piano, which was arranged most considerately, so that you faced the dancers, and you could enjoy watching them as you played. This was my forte, dance music. In Plantersville they said I could make any one dance, and it gave me almost as much pleasure as dancing itself. Soon the floor was full of whirling couples, and I had a chance to see how many of them I knew and how many

I didn't know. Alas, the latter were vastly in the majority, but, I reflected with joy, when ever I had no partner, *I could play.* So when Miss Heyward came to relieve me I was in a gale of spirits, and C. came to claim a promised dance; so I went through that, though with reluctance, for he was not as good a dancer as he had been fighter. I got on *tant bien que mal*, until glasses of water were handed round and people began to settle for "the German." This was unknown to me, and I watched the bringing in of chairs and the happy couples placing themselves around the big room. Mr. Joe Manigault, a great society man and exquisite dancer from "before the War," was to lead. Nearly all the chairs were filled and I was still at the piano. Then I saw Mr. M. take one young man after another into the piazza and walk them up and down, and I knew he was trying to induce them to let him present them to me so that they could ask me for the German. I could see them glance at me surreptitiously through the window, while walking. One after another returned to the room, not having yielded to Mr. M. At last, he found one who valiantly came forward, was introduced and asked for the pleasure, and I accepted with great alacrity, and never began to

tease him about having ignominiously allowed
Mr. M. to choose his partner for him until the
German was well under way. And then I pointed
to the row of "stags," as they were called who
would not take partners, relying on being "taken
out," being all good dancers. Then between
times they could retire to the piazza and smoke.
He was bright and able to answer my ungracious
attacks, so that I got quite as good as I gave.
Add to this that, as soon as any one danced with
me, being thrown together in the figures of the
German, they always wanted to dance with me
again, and soon all the stags came up and were
introduced, eager to be "taken out" by me; but
nay, nay, I let them ornament the wall as far as
I was concerned. And oh I had a glorious time,
Mr. M. himself selecting me very often to lead the
figures with him. He had to tell me just what to
do, but I soon learned, and when it was my turn
to play he would not let me, but suggested to one
sweet quiet girl that played very well that she
should take my turn, saying I had played twice
my share earlier in the evening. We broke up at 12
exactly, as all the men are working hard and must
get their sleep. They have formed a Cotillion
Club and are going to give a dance once a month

and I have been asked by three men for the next German. My ears are so sore from my adornments that I don't think I will wear them again, though they are beautiful. Aunt was delighted with my account of the party, and laughed and chuckled over my first German partner, saying, "Men are fools, and always will be."

CHAPTER XXIX

MAMMA'S SCHOOL

Dec. 1st, 1865.

PREPARATIONS for the school are going on apace. We have moved into our house and it is too beautiful. I had forgotten how lovely it was. Fortunately, the beautiful paper in the second floor, the two drawing rooms and Mamma's room, has not been at all injured. The school is to open Jan. 1st and, strange to say, Mamma is receiving letters from all over the State asking terms etc. I thought there would be no applications, every one being so ruined by the War, but Mamma's name and personality make people anxious to give their daughters the benefit of her influence; and, I suppose, the people in the cotton country are not so completely ruined and without money as we rice planters of the low country are. Be it as it may, the limit Mamma put of ten boarding pupils is nearly reached already. My cousin, Marianna Porcher, will be the head teacher of French and Literature; she is wonderfully clever; I will have the younger girls, and I certainly will have my hands full, for there are a great many applications for the entry of day-scholars of the younger set. Mamma will teach all the classes of History, for which she is admirably fitted. Prof. Gibbes from the Charleston College will teach Mathematics and Latin to the advanced scholars; but I want Mlle. Le Prince, who is a first class French teacher, engaged to live in the house as well as teach. There is no way of learning French equal to speaking it. But Mamma very truly says we must go slowly, and be sure we are making, before we expand. I am frightened to death. I know girls and have been to Boarding School and Mamma's plan of no rules except those of an ordinary well-ordered, well-conducted home, seems to me perfectly impracticable; but, having once said that, I do not dare argue the matter. I am amazed to see how clever Mamma is. She wanted to send C. to College in Virginia, his constitution has been much injured by the heavy marching and privation endured in the Army at 16. Carrying that heavy knapsack on those killing, long marches without food has given him a stoop and a weary look in his beautiful hazel eyes; but it was impossible for her to borrow the $200.00 necessary to send him. She thought the change of climate from this relaxing low country air would do him good, and enable him to build up; but, as she could not get the money, she has placed him at the Charleston College, and I am truly thankful to have him at home. Only, restless, Cassandra-like, I see a problem ahead; he is so very good-looking!

March 21st, 1866. Here we are, almost at the end of our first three months of school, and it has been and is a grand success! I have not had time to write a line here because every second of my time is occupied, and oh, I am so happy! In the first place, I find I can teach! And I love it! I have a class of thirteen girls ranging from twelve to fifteen, and, if you please, I teach them everything! except history which Mamma teaches. They are most of them very bright, delightful girls, and mind my least word, even look. Only once have I had any trouble. I kept a girl in for an hour after school because she had not pretended to study her lesson that day, and the next day I had a note from her Mother to say that she was shocked at her daughter being singled out for punishment, and requesting that it should not happen again. I returned a note saying that I also requested earnestly that it should not happen again, that M. come to her class without having studied her lesson; should it happen a second time, the punishment would have to be much more severe. I had no reply to that, but M., who is very bright tho' very spoiled, thought wisest to study in future. A Mother, who had taught in her youth and who knew of this passage at arms, wrote me a note of sympathy, saying, "A teacher must be prepared to swallow buckets full of adders." This was so very strong and so beyond my experience, that I did not answer it, and thus far I can truly say I have not swallowed a single mosquito even.

I have a little time today and I want to put down what I do every day, I really have not added it up even in my mind. First of all, I trim and fill all the lamps, twenty in all, for we have no light but kerosene in the house; the fixtures are all there, but gas is so expensive; then I practise a half hour before going into school at nine; school lasts until two; there is no general recess, each class going into the garden for their recess at a different time; then I give one or two music lessons every day, that takes more out of me than anything. Once a week, Mr. Hambruch gives me a lesson, from pure goodness and love of music; for, of course, I could not afford it. He taught me for years when I was young, and when he offered to give me a spare hour he had, I was too glad. Yesterday I went to him almost crying, and told him how badly I felt at taking money for girls who were not learning any thing. He laughed and answered, "Oh, Miss A., you must not mind that. We music teachers, if we only taught the ones that learn, we would starve."

That was a great surprise and consolation to me, for he is the very best music teacher in Charleston, and I was so proud of his saying, "We music teachers." Of course I only charge a quarter of what he charges for lessons and people have so little money that I have a good many pupils, as Mr. H. was so good as to give me a certificate as to my capacity to teach. I make every stitch of clothing that I wear, and that takes up every spare moment; add to all this that I go into society, and enjoy myself fiercely.

We have ten delightful girls as boarding pupils, from all over the State. They are preternaturally well behaved, and Mamma's plan of its being really a home, with no rules, is succeeding perfectly. My dear, pretty little sister is a kind of lead horse in the team, and as she walks straight the rest follow. But they really are exceptionally nice ladylike girls who treat Mamma like a queen.

C. is the greatest help to Mamma, and, so far,

has kept his eyes to himself. He is a wonder. He does all the marketing on his way to College! And that is no small thing. Beef is 50 c. a pound and mutton in proportion. C. sits at the foot of the table and carves and helps one dish of meat while Mamma carves the other. He is as solemn and well behaved as a judge, and though the girls adore him, it is in secret, so all goes well.

The "Young Ladies," contrary to all my ideas, are allowed to receive visitors Friday, Saturday and Sunday evenings, when J. and I also have visitors, and Mamma sits in the room, sometimes talking with us, sometimes reading; but the evenings are very gay and pleasant, and, I am forced to admit, have no demoralizing effect. On the contrary, their manners and deportment have visibly improved.

Mamma looks perfectly lovely, as she sits reading in her plain black frock and widow's cap. She is a little over fifty, but her hair is brown and curly and her complexion as smooth and unwrinkled as a girl's, only she is very white and seldom has a colour, as she used to do. She is a great reader and one of my friends, who has a good library and also reviews the new books, and so gets them, brings her some book of great interest every time he comes to make me a visit, and they talk a great deal together. Sometimes I get quite jealous, for I do not read deep books. I mean I would not care to if I had time. I never have time to read at all.

I must explain here how the great and unexpected pleasure of going into society came to me. I had quite given up all hope of that joy, for once when I asked mamma about my going out sometimes, she seemed quite shocked, as though it were an absolute impossibility, so I never said anything more about it. But after the school was well started, the son of my father's friend, Nicholas Williams (the same whose family had been so wonderfully good and generous to us, lending us Crowley Hill as a home for the whole war, and lavishing the products of their farm and garden upon us), brought his two beautiful daughters, one barely fifteen, the other seventeen; and Mrs. Williams asked my mother to receive them for French, literature, and history only, and expressed the wish that they should go into society, as much as practicable, as their time would not be fully occupied by their studies. My mother consented, and these delightful girls came, Serena a queenly brunette and Mary a madonna-faced blonde, but it was not wise to trust too much to that demure expression. When the first invitations came to a ball for us all, mamma came to me and said: "Bessie, you will have to go and chaperon the girls, for after the work of the day I am quite unequal to going out and sitting up half the night."

I tried not to show my delight too plainly, but answered quietly, that I would do my best in the new rôle of chaperon. We went to the ball, and I was very proud of my beauties, and their lovely clothes. The acting chaperon was very small, very thin, and dressed in a frock she had made herself in between times, a little over twenty, and nobody thought that she would be able to manage the responsibilities, for the girls were great belles from the first moment, but there never was the least difficulty or friction; they were well-bred, well-trained girls, accustomed to recognize and yield to authority; which was for the moment represented in the person of their very small, very plain chaperon. I soon grew very fond of them. They called me "Miss Allston" most carefully. Altogether the going into society with them was just the last thing necessary to fill my cup of happiness to the brim. My every faculty was in full use, and the going out and dancing, instead of being a fatigue, took away all sense of fatigue; I myself have no doubt but that rhythmic motion to music is one of the most restful things in the world. I feel quite sure that in the end this will be recognized by the medical profession as the best cure for nervous diseases.

CHAPTER XXX

THE SCHOOL A SUCCESS

Charleston, January, 1867.

WE are now well on in the second year of the school, and it is no longer an experiment but a great success. Mamma's methods and judgment have been fully justified. The "young Ladies" have behaved entirely like young ladies, and never done any of the things I feared. I have the delight of having Mlle. Le Prince established in the house, and French the language of the school, in a modified way, that is, there are no punishments for speaking English, but if a girl is really in earnest about learning, she speaks French, and if she is not it does not matter. I am getting to delight in teaching, and my little class learns amazingly.

April, '67. I have had a grand winter; Mary and Serena came for a long visit and went out during the season. They had the most beautiful Paris ball-dresses. It is impossible to describe the effect produced by these beautiful women in their beautiful costumes.

Every one was nicely dressed, for all the girls

and their mothers had become expert dressmakers, with few exceptions. But the frocks were generally of the simplest muslins, sweet and fresh, but not such as would be worn in the great world to a full-dress ball; and when these creations, which would have been thought brilliant in any ballroom burst upon us, we were filled with admiration and wonder.

I had risen to the dignity of two silk dresses this year, and felt very grand before the appearance of the Paris toilets. At the beginning of the war, mamma had packed all of Della's and her best clothes, for which she knew they would have no use while refugees, in two large trunks, and they had been sent up the Pee Dee River to Morven in a flat with a load of rice. The flat had struck a snag and sunk, and the trunks had remained under water a long time, so that almost everything was ruined, but in looking over the mass of mildewed stuffs, I found two dresses of mamma's, which I asked her to give me, as I thought I could make something of them. One was a very heavy thick black silk, with stripes of satin about two inches wide, every two inches apart, the stripes running across, or bayadere, as it was called then. But this was no longer the fashion; so I ripped up the very ample full skirt, and after washing it three times to get off the stains of the muddy river water in which it had lain so long, I sewed the breadths together, matching the stripes so exactly that no one could imagine that it had been done. Then I cut the most beautiful long skirt by a Paris pattern, gored like an umbrella at the top, and flaring out into the most wonderful long train, which was stiffened with buckram, so that as you danced it slid along the waxed floor, even when your partner backed you all over the room; then the low-necked waist, which did fit beautifully, was trimmed with thread lace, and was sewed to the skirt. I thought the effect was regal. The other was a very heavy purple satin brocaded so as to make the effect of a purple satin covered with black lace. This was harder to wash and cleanse than the black, but I worked at it in the holidays, and ended by succeeding in making it too a thing of beauty, and felt that I was provided with apparel suitable to my character as chaperon.

My friends were more beautiful than ever this season. I had become perfectly devoted to Serena, and she had showed that she returned the feeling, for in sending to Paris for their season's toilets she had sent for six beautifully fine pock-et-handkerchiefs for me, with my monogram most elaborately embroidered on them, the finest, most beautiful handkerchiefs I have had in my long life, I have one still just as a memento of her affection; beauty, spoiled and adored by men as she was, she had to divert some of the cotton money sent to Paris from her own finery to give me this delight.

They were not at school this year, and I found it much harder to maintain my authority and dignity with them. Serena was terribly strong, and one day when she wanted to do something to which I would not consent, she came into my room, to make a last appeal to me; I was only half dressed, and she picked me up and threw me up in the air, and as she caught me, said: "Now will you let me?" I panted out: "Now less than ever." She threw me up once more and left the room. There was a tale of her wishing to get her father's consent to some plan, and holding him over the banister of the second-story piazza, saying she would drop him unless he yielded to her will; of course she did not get her wish. She was a grand woman, and no wonder she counted her victims by scores.

I wish I had time to tell of my many friends; they were all such nice men, who had fought through the war, and now were not ashamed to take any kind of honest work to enable them to help their mothers and sisters. There were literally butchers and bakers, and candlestick-makers, but all thorough, true gentlemen, and most of them beautiful dancers. The only public balls we had that year were the three balls given by the Cotillion Club. They were in the South Carolina Hall, with a fine waxed floor and good band of music, but very mild refreshments.

The private parties were too delightful; the young men of the family giving the party always waxed the floor, and they became experts in doing it, and that was really the sole thing absolutely necessary to the success of a party. We were sure of good music, for there were four or five girls going into society that played delightfully for dancing. The refreshments generally consisted of rolls, handed in dishes of exquisite china, and water in very dainty glasses. At one or two houses we had the rare treat of coffee, but that did not often happen, and when the rolls appeared just before the German, they were very welcome, and greatly enjoyed, for we were all working hard,

[320]

and living none too high. In the winter the only recreation, except the dancing, was walking on the Battery in the afternoon. We made engagements for this, just as we did for a German, generally with girl friends, for the men at work did not get off for the afternoons. A run on the Battery in the early dusk, or just at sunset, after a hard day's teaching was something heavenly, and when you had a friend near enough to enjoy silence nothing could be more perfect. Before the war my father never let us walk on the Battery on Sunday afternoon, for he said it was only fair for the darkies to have it that evening, and after the war no one walked there that afternoon, for it was thronged with negroes. The regular promenade for us that afternoon after church, for every one went to church morning and afternoon in those days, was down a very narrow, rough pavement to the west end of Tradd Street, to what was then Chisolm's Mill, beyond all the houses, where the street was simply a roadway, with the marsh behind, and the broad salt river in front. Along the road piles of logs and lumber had been dumped here and there. To this spot the élite of Charleston wended their way, lads and lasses, two and two, and sat on the logs in place of benches, and watched the sun slowly sink into the gorgeous clouds, which swallowed it up all too quickly, proclaiming the end of our happy day of REST. Many a momentous conversation was murmured on those logs, with the strong, pungent smell of the marshes borne to us by the brisk, fresh breezes. Many a life contract was sealed there. Somehow it was easier to speak freely in those surroundings, all telling of work and toil, no beauty but God's great lavish glory of sun and clouds and river and sky. What mattered money and income and fashion? Surely to love God and work and do your duty to the best of your ability, holding the strong, firm hand of the woman you loved, was to make the best of your life, and would insure a blessing upon it.

No one will ever know how many troths were plighted there, nor how many lives, starting out with that simple, childlike faith, in the saving power of love and duty (that word so greatly scorned now), were justified in their confidence, and were noble and happy, and have brought up families of whom they may well be proud. I can never forget the shock of my first proposal, which took place down there. I had worked so hard before I left the country to prevent the asking of that question, and had succeeded so well, knowing all

the time in my secret heart that I had done so
because I doubted my power to say no with suffi-
cient firmness if the fateful words were spoken,
had put all such thoughts out of my mind entirely;
I went out as a chaperon, enjoying myself as a
married woman would do; I knew there was only
one man in the world that I would ever marry,
and not quite sure that I could even marry him,
but I forgot that other people did not know that.
I had a great deal of attention and a great many
friends, but never thought of them as possible
lovers; so when one evening, sitting on a pile of
squared logs which were far from comfortable,
watching the tide come in, with the most glorious
sunset clouds reflected in the water, and we had
stopped talking for some time, and my thoughts
were far away, Mr. Blank asked me to marry him,
I just gasped with horror and exclaimed: "Oh,
how awful! How could you spoil all our delightful friendship in this way! I am so distressed!"
But he said: "Miss Bessie, this is very extraordinary conduct on your part! What did you think
that I was coming to see you all the time for, and
playing chess regularly once a week for, and following you.about all the time at the parties, and
doing everything in the world I could for you for?

[323]

I have never cared for any one else, and I never thought you could fail to understand my devotion."

"Oh," I repeated, "it is too awful! You know, your dear sister was my best friend, and I liked you because of that, and I thought that was what made you like me, and I liked to be with you because you looked like her and reminded me of her; I have missed her so ever since she died. But now I see how blind and selfish I have been." We had an awful walk home and parted at the steps, and he never came to see me again.

As the days passed and he did not come to see me, mademoiselle, who had become devoted to me and watched my visitors with intense interest, said to me: "Ou est donc ce bon M. Blanc? Il ne vient plus! J'espère que vous ne l'avez pas renvoyé! Il etait si bel homme, et si gentil! Je ne pense pas que vous ayez la chance d'attirer un si bon parti encore!"

This experience was a blow, and destroyed my confidence in and enjoyment of my friends; my eyes had been opened, and I was more careful in accepting men's friendship as if they were girls. Nearly all the men in town fell victims to my beautiful friends, and when they left to go to their new home in Virginia things were very flat, and the men very gloomy. My diary is at an end and I am very hazy and uncertain about dates. When we went this summer for the holidays up to my brother, at the log house in Plantersville, we took Mlle. le Prince with us, as she had nowhere to go, and I devoted a good deal of my time to studying French with her. We read "Les Travailleurs de la Mer," and I remember very distinctly her disgust and disappointment; she would exclaim: "Appeler cela un roman ! Ou est donc l'amour ?" Never having had any love-affair of her own, she was unwilling to read any book which did not supply her craving for love-stories, and she saw no beauty in Victor Hugo's masterpiece.

I cannot be sure, but I think it was this winter that General Sickles was put in command of Charleston. He took a big house in Charlotte Street, and soon after he got established there he brought his little daughter to mamma and asked to enter her at the school as a day-scholar, and mamma accepted her pleasantly as such. But it made quite a commotion; the feeling of many in the community was that mamma should have refused to take her. Those who were so bold as to speak to her on the subject were careful not to repeat their indiscretion. One lady, however, was bold enough to say that she did not desire such association for her daughter, and my mother told her then she had best remove her daughter from school, which she did. There never was a more pathetic little figure than that of the new scholar; very pale, very thin and tall, about ten she looked, and dressed in the deepest, plainest black, with none of the natural gaiety of a child; it was said she had just lost her mother, but there was no way of getting behind the wall of childish reserve which this young spirit had been able to build around her inner being. My mother taught her altogether herself, for she did not fit into any of the classes, and mamma was deeply interested in her.

The last year we were in Charleston the St. Cecilia Society began to revive, and determined to give two balls. This was a great event, and every one began to think about a ball dress. I, being like the immortal Mrs. Gilpin, who, "though on pleasure bent, had a frugal mind," had bought a good piece of white alpaca, and constructed a frock of that, trimmed with handsome scarlet silk-velvet ribbon, which had trimmed an opera-cloak of my sister's, made in Paris, which had gone down in the river with the other fine clothes. It was a miracle that the velvet survived the ordeal, and was still beautiful after being steamed, and I was delighted with my frock when it was finished. Mamma had not ever seemed to think about my clothes, but the idea of a St. Cecilia Ball roused her to ask: "Bessie, have you a suitable dress for the approaching ball?"

"Yes, mamma, I have a very nice frock."

"What is it?"

"A white alpaca trimmed with red velvet, and I have covered my slippers with red velvet to match."

Mamma exclaimed in horror: "An alpaca dress for a St. Cecilia Ball! Impossible! I cannot consent to your going so unsuitably dressed."

Then I burst out most improperly: "It is too late now to say that. I have spent my hard-earned money for the frock, and it is finished. I got it because it would last better than a muslin, and when it gets dirty I can have it dyed for a day frock. You used to take great interest in Della's clothes and choose them all, because she was pretty, but as I am ugly you have never cared what I put on."

Poor mamma was terribly shocked, and said so; then she said: "I certainly will see that you have a proper outfit for this occasion."

True to her word, she went out, bought and had made by Mrs. Cummings, the best dressmaker in town, a real ball dress. White tulle over white silk, and trimmed with wreaths of little fine white flowers. When I went to try it on I could scarcely believe my eyes, and found it hard to sleep that night for thinking of it. Mrs. Cummings promised to have it sent by seven o'clock Thursday, the night of the ball. I waited and looked anxiously; eight came, no dress, and finally at nine I sent the others off to the ball and went to bed. I felt I had been well punished for my wicked outburst of temper; but perhaps few can understand how I suffered, for few, I think, have the intense love of pleasure which I had in my youth. I could, and did, throw myself, heart and soul into my work, whatever it was, but I threw myself with equal vehemence into my play when the work was over. In two weeks' time came the next St. Cecilia, and I went and wore my beautiful ball dress, but I had a very chastened feeling all the evening. The frock was a dream, quite short, with little pleatings of tulle, from the waist to the bottom; the waist fitted perfectly, and mamma had fulfilled her promise of an outfit, for she had bought white kid slippers (one and a half was then my number) and a pair of white kid gloves, something I had never even dreamed of; so for once I was properly attired according to the ideas of the great world, and mamma was very pleased when I went to show myself to her before going. We still walked to all entertainments in our boots, our slippers, carefully wrapped up, being intrusted to our escort, who received them with a kind of reverence mingled with joy, at having committed to his care a part of one's vital belongings. This was only for real balls, however; at the little informal dances which we had very often, we danced in our walking shoes, always waxing the soles thoroughly before going into the dancing-room. This important service was also rendered by one's escort, and was regarded almost in the light of an accolade. In the rather laborious life that I led, never any fire in my bedroom, never any hot water, I suffered terribly from chilblains, and my hands and feet were often greatly swollen, so that I could not get on my shoes; then, instead of staying away, I asked mamma if she would lend me her best shoes. This was mamma's only extravagance; she was a very tall woman with beautiful hands and feet, long and narrow, and common shoes did not fit her at all, so she had her boots made to order, at what to us seemed an enormous price; she wore fives, much too long for her, as she liked them that way, but fitting perfectly in every other way. I could see that it was a supreme sacrifice on her part to lend me those, her most precious possession, but she consented, and I went off to a dance at the Dessaussure's, arrayed in my black silk and mamma's shoes, and enjoyed my comfortable feet immensely; I had stuffed the toes with cotton, as it was only in the length they were too big, and when people stepped on my foot, as was often the case that first evening that I wore them, as I had not got accustomed to managing feet so much longer than usual, they would apologize humbly and hope they had not hurt me too badly, I always answered: "You have not hurt me at all; that was only my shoe you stepped on, not my foot" — to their great amusement. One day a man said: "I was asked a conundrum that is going the rounds last night: what young lady has the biggest shoe and the smallest foot in town?" All this is very trivial and very silly, but as I make the effort to recall the past, all these foolish details come, and I just put them down.

CHAPTER XXXI

1868

THIS was a very happy year to me and to mamma. My little sister made her début, and she was so pretty and so charming that she was greatly admired and had a great many adorers. This added immensely to my pleasure in going out, and I think it was a great relief to mamma to have another very pretty daughter to be proud of. Two or three of the older girls were allowed to go to parties, too, and they were a charming lot, abounding in youth and joy. I cannot remember all, but some I was especially fond of come to me: Rosa Evans, a tiny little thing, as bright as a steel trap, with very fair skin and brown hair almost touching the floor, and so thick that it was hard for her to dispose of it on her small head; she had many serious admirers; she came from Society Hill, where every one had been so good to us during the war; Sophie Bonham, a charmingly pretty brunette, as quiet as a mouse, but none the less having many admirers, Charley and herself being great friends, he having by a miracle escaped without a broken heart from the all-conquering Serena; then came Maggie Jordan, who though not nearly so handsome, looked very like her sister Victoria, who had been one of the beauties of madame's school when I was a little girl, and who was blown up on a steamer on the Mississippi when on her wedding-trip. I can remember the faces and individualities of others, but their names are too vague to attempt to record them. All this time I was too happy and too busy sometimes to be able to sleep! It was the greatest joy to me to have Jinty going out with me, and to see her so much admired; she had many charming steadies, and then we had some friends in common; I remember at this moment one man, older than the majority of our friends, Bayard Clinch, such a delightful man; he was her admirer but my friend. Altogether we had a very gay time. My own special friend was working so hard on the rice-plantation in the country that he did not very often get to town, and then, though I always knew when I entered a ballroom if he was there, without seeing him, by a queer little feeling, I always treated him with great coolness and never gave him more than one dance in an evening, for there were two kind of people I could not bear to dance with — the people whom I disliked and those I liked too much, and he was the only one in the second class. Besides, he had learned to dance in Germany, and had practised it at Heidelberg, and shot about the floor in an extraordinary manner, which endangered the equilibrium of the quiet couples, and that made me furious.

Charley was a beautiful dancer, and very popular, and I am afraid something of a flirt, with his great, sleepy, hazel eyes, but he was most sedate as an escort, as solemn as a judge, and the girls minded his injunctions absolutely in all social matters, which was a great mercy, for the etiquette in their home towns was by no means as strict as that dictated by St. Cecilia standards.

Before the school term was over this spring I received an invitation from Mrs. David Williams, to spend two months with Serena and Mary at their farm near Staunton, Virginia, which I accepted with delight, and began the preparation at once for my summer outfit, which would have to be a little more elaborate than what I prepared for a summer at Plantersville. When the time came for leaving, my uncle Chancellor Lesesne took me to the station and put me on the train. He gave me many directions as to my conduct on

[333]

the journey, as it was looked upon as a very hazardous departure from custom for me to make the journey alone; among other charges that he gave he said: "My dear niece, let nothing induce you to let a young man speak to you! It would be most improper to enter into conversation with any man, but the natural questions which you might have to ask of an official of the road, whom you will recognize by his uniform." Then he bade me an affectionate and solemn farewell, which started me with a lump in my throat. The end of the eight months of teaching, not to speak of my other activities, always found me in a shattered condition. Toward the end of the last month the dropping of a slate startled me into disgraceful tears, which were almost impossible to stop. I used to be quite touched at the great care the girls took not to drop a book or even a pencil, and those who had annoyed me the most by their recklessness in this respect were the most careful now; this was wonderful, for I was awfully cross and irritable. After settling myself in my place, and getting out my book and fan and everything else I could possibly need, Uncle Henry's words came to my mind with renewed force. I had insisted that I was not at all afraid, and would rather travel alone than waste two weeks of my

good holiday and invitation, waiting until a party
was going on to Virginia, who said they would take
charge of me. But Uncle Henry had succeeded
in making me feel that I was courting danger, dis-
aster, and insult, and my strained nerves were delighted to seize and elaborate that theme, so that
when we got to the place where I had to change
cars for Staunton (I am not sure, but I think it
was Alexandria), I got out and stood by my trunk
(which had to be rechecked here) in perfect despair; a very nice-looking, gentlemanly young man
came up and said: "Can I do anything for you?"
With the last remnants of composure, I said, "No,
thank you," and watched him with dismay disappear into the car. At last the conductor came
and stood a second at the door of the car and
called: "All 'board!" I made a dart to the car,
saying to myself, "Let the trunk go; I don't
care," and got up the steps and into the car, to
find not a seat, so I stood in the middle of the
crowded car, with my heavy blue veil down to
conceal the marks of agitation on my face, and
my valise in my hand. Fortunately, the conductor rushed through, and I managed to say:
"My trunk is out there." In his great haste he
looked where I pointed, rushed to the baggage-
car and sent two men, who ran, seized the trunk,

and pitched it aboard just as the train started. The conductor came back and asked me why under the sun I had not spoken to him before, "that it was a very near thing, and that if the trunk had been left there, in all probability it would never have been seen again, as things were pretty unsettled in these parts." I was in no condition to enter into conversation; my throat ached so that when I tried to tell the man that I had not spoken to him because I had not seen him, he had trouble in understanding me. The rest of my journey was short, fortunately, and my hearty reception restored my equanimity, but it was some time before I had recovered my voice and spirits enough to be able to narrate all my experiences, to the great amusement of the party. I tell all this because it is hard to believe that such a state of things could have ever been possible, when we see the ease and aplomb with which very young girls move about the world, from end to end literally. But that was fifty-three years ago, and surely there is no one who would not say that we have made a wonderful advance in sense.

The home life of this family always remains in my mind as a beautiful picture, each member doing his or her own part as perfectly as it could be done. Mr. Williams had shown his foresight and common sense in an uncommon way, for during the war, when it was by no means necessary, as they were wealthy, he had insisted that his daughters (who were attending a school kept by the De Choiseul family and were having a first-class education) should be taught to cook and to wash, for he said that to him it seemed likely that they would have much more use for these domestic arts than for the more ornamental branches; the combination had been altogether charming. Finding his property all gone, making it impossible to spend his winters in Florida and the summers in the mountains at their beautiful place at Flat Rock, he determined to sell both these delightful homes, not being willing for his family to live altogether in the enervating climate of Florida, and there was no chance of making a living at Flat Rock. So he sold them and bought a farm in Virginia, where they could spend winter and summer in a fine climate, and where he could cultivate the land and make a living. It had been almost impossible to bring on their handsome furniture, and it would have been most unsuitable to this farmhouse, so he had a workshop in which he manufactured the most delightful rustic chairs and couches and dressing-tables, which with pretty chintz cushions and curtains made the interior fascinating and unique. I would like to run on and give a full description of my perfect visit; but I must hasten to a close; only one little thing I must tell. Soon after I arrived we were invited to a dance. As I was sitting up in my room, reading, as I always did in the morning while the girls went to do their respective duties in the household — for they would not let me help in the smallest way, saying I was there for rest and must have it, and after a short struggle I gave in completely — Serena came in and asked what I was going to wear to the dance that night; I answered, my barège frock. "Oh, no, wear your white muslin, please." I answered truly that it was not fresh enough, as I had worn it constantly before leaving home and had not had time to have it done up. Nothing would content her until I took it out for her to look at; then, to my surprise, she said: "Why, that is quite fresh enough; I will take it down for Mollie to smooth, and it will do nicely." Of course I yielded, as I always did to Serena in the end, but I wondered over it, for the dress was really dirty. In the afternoon, when I came up to get ready, there was my frock spread out on the bed, beautifully done up! I flew down to the kitchen to thank Mollie, but she said: "You needn't to thank me, ma'am; shure an' 'twas Miss

Serena as don it; she washed it, an' she starched it, and she i'oned it, an' her just drippin' with the sweat." I was overcome; to think of this beauty and belle, adored and spoiled by so many, doing this in order that her work-weary, plain little friend should look her best, for the barège was a pretty, nice new frock, but she did not think as becoming. I think such friendship is rare. I was to go to Baltimore for a short visit when I left the farm, and it was decided that I needed another frock; after discussing the important matter thoroughly Mrs. Williams said she thought a black silk was what I should have; I quailed at the expense of such a thing, but she said: "Bessie, you send and buy the silk and I will make it up." So I sent and got ten yards of beautiful black silk, and my wonderful hostess cut, fitted, and made a most stylish walking-suit, the very joy of my heart. Of course, I helped with the sewing, but I could never have undertaken so handsome a costume alone. I left my dear friends with tears; it was leaving peace and joy and love behind.

CHAPTER XXXII

CHICORA WOOD

March, 1869.

I AM holding on to every moment of my full happy life, for this is to be our last year in Charleston. Mamma has applied for her dower, and when it is assigned her, we will move into the country, as Charlie is to graduate this spring at the college, and Jinty's education is complete, and Mamma prefers the country where Charlie can make a living by planting rice. Every one is happy over it but me; I cannot bear the thought of giving up my full life; but I try not to think about it until it comes, but to enjoy the present without alloy. Anyway we would have to give up this beautiful house for the creditors of the estate want to sell it.

I have so many delightful friends; one specially who has actually taught me to love poetry, by his persistence in reading it to me. I do believe I have always liked it in my heart, for among my most cherished books from the time I was four-teen are Chaucer's Canterbury Tales given me by my first hero Cousin Johnston Pettigrew, and a

little fat leather-bound copy of Homer's Iliad, I
never moved without these two. Then I liked
Evangeline, and Hiawatha, but I never could get
up any enthusiasm for The Lady of the Lake, so
I had got into the habit of saying with a certain
pride that I did not like poetry.

April. Every Friday evening Mr. Sass comes
and we read Italian together, which is delightful.
I have studied a little alone, and when I was
about thirteen, to every one's great amusement,
I used to take an hour's lesson in the afternoon,
once a week, from M. Pose. I have always loved
languages and Italian is especially beautiful, and in
singing it is such a help to know it. Now we are
reading Goldoni's plays, and the Italian is so simple, it is very easy to read, very different from the
Jerusalem, which we read first. My mind is so
eager for knowledge, it is positively uncanny, it
springs forward so to meet things, I fear me it is
more than usually true of me that "Knowledge
comes but wisdom lingers."

I need ballast so much, if I had only had a
man's education. A good course of mathematics
under a severe master would help me greatly, and
I need help.

The only form of amusement that the young

men could afford was boating, and soon after we began the school, Charlie sent to the plantation and got Brother to send down to him one of the rowboats. Rainbow, the pride of the plantation, had been lent to the Confederate Government, for use on the fortifications and we never got her back, but Brother sent the next best and it was a fine rowboat. Charlie named it the Countess, and he and his friends had great pleasure in her; Tom Frost, Arthur Mazyck, William Jervey, James Lesesne and himself were the crew, and they invited their girl friends to the most delightful moonlight rows. They went on long fishing trips on Saturdays and all their holidays, coming back happy but their faces pealing from sunburn. The exercise kept them in good health and spirits.

May, 1869. Things are moving on rapidly. When Mamma applied for her dower, she said she would take a sixth of the real estate in fee simple, instead of a third for life only; she has received information that the creditors appointed a board of Appraisers, to value the property and decide, and after careful valuation they have decided that the plantation, Chicora Wood, where she has always lived will constitute a sixth of the land in value, and have awarded her that. It is too delightful!

and she is so happy, and we are all so happy, for the idea of giving up Chicora was dreadful, and we feared they would think it too valuable for a sixth. It has all to be repaired as the house is all torn to pieces, but Mamma has been so wonderful that she has invested more than a thousand dollars every year of the school, and she has begged Brother to engage carpenters and begin the restoration of the house and out-buildings at once, so that it will be ready for us next winter. I only wish my heart was not so heavy about going.

The packing up of all our belongings was a tremendous business, but in this as in everything else Charley was most efficient, and he did it with a good heart, as it was the greatest happiness to him that we were moving back to Chicora, and that he was going to plant the place. Jinty was also perfectly happy, the thought of being able to live on horseback once more filled her with joy. I, only, was downhearted; to me human nature had become more interesting than plain nature, and people more fascinating than plants. So I determined to apply for a place as music-teacher in the town of Union, S. C., which had been held by a very charming friend of mine who played beautifully, Caro Ravenel. The family did not approve of my doing this as mamma thought I needed rest; anyway, we were to go to the pineland for the summer and I would not have to leave for Union until the autumn.

I remember well the last Sunday we were to be in Charleston; during the service I was so moved that I had to put down my heavy veil to conceal my tears!

Just at this time a most wonderful thing happened: mamma got a letter from our cousin, John Earl Allston, of Brooklyn, N. Y., saying:

"MY DEAR COUSIN:

"I have placed to your credit in the Bank of Charleston the sum of $5,000, which I hope will be useful to you.

"You need feel no sense of obligation in receiving it, for it is not one-half of what my Cousin Robert, your husband, did for me and mine in the past. When my mother's house was to be sold over her head, he bought it in and gave it to her, and many other things he did for us, and it is a great pleasure to me to be able to do this for his widow and family."

Of course, this was as great a blessing as it was a surprise. It so happened that my mother had, in looking over some old papers recently, come upon a letter to my father, with a memorandum on the back in papa's handwriting: "Application from John E. Allston, for an increase in the amount of allowance made to his brother Washington, as his health is much worse, and the expenses heavier; have directed that it be in future $500, instead of $300, as heretofore." But she knew nothing about the purchase of the home.

It was too wonderful that this great good luck and mercy should come to us just at this moment, when it would enable mamma to buy things necessary to the beginning of the planting; for she not only had to repair the house at Chicora, but she would have to buy in her own horses and cows and oxen (which last are absolutely necessary to ploughing the rice-lands, as their cloven hoofs do not sink in the boggy land, in which a horse would go down hopelessly); also ploughs and harrows and wagons and carriages, all had to be paid for; so dear, unknown Cousin John had chosen the psychic moment to appear as *deus ex machina*.

Afterward Cousin John visited mamma at Chicora Wood, and we came to know and love him. He told with the most beautiful simplicity of the long and terrible struggle he had to make a living; like many an Allston he lacked entirely the commercial instinct, and it was much easier for him to spend money than to make it; but he had managed to have a home in Brooklyn, and support his wife and one daughter in very moderate comfort, until this adored only child reached the age of sixteen; then she grew pale and thin, without life, or spirit, or appetite, and terror seized the parents; the doctor called in said: "She must travel; this city air is killing her. Take her away at once to the mountains, and you may save her." He had prescribed what to him seemed simple, but to the distracted father, who was straining every nerve just to provide daily food, it was utterly out of reach!

John Earl Allston had a very rich uncle, his mother's brother, but once in the past, being in distress for money, he had written to ask a loan from him, not a large sum, and promising to pay by a certain date, when his income should come next. He not only did not receive the loan, but the refusal was almost insulting, to the effect that he, the uncle, had worked for his money, and he strongly advised his nephew to do the same, and not try to borrow. So Cousin John knew there was no use to apply to him again, and there was no one else; the war was going on, and so my father was not accessible, and he had just to watch his darling fade away and die. Then his wife was so agonized over the misery of seeing death creep nearer and nearer and finally take her lovely child, that her health gave way. The doctor when called made the same prescription: "The only way to save her is to give her change of air and scene." As before, this was impossible, and she soon was laid beside her child. About a year after Cousin John was left desolate and alone, the uncle died, and he was notified that he had inherited a fortune! It was most terrible to him. All that money, one hundredth part of which could have saved his beloved wife and daughter, to spend on himself alone!

It was truly dust and ashes, and intensified his sorrow. Then, when he found himself getting bitter and unlike himself, he called a halt. "Cousin," he said, "I made up my mind to spend my time in giving away my money while I was alive, and have at least the enjoyment of making people happy by a little timely present, and you don't know how their letters have helped me, for I find so many to whom a few thousand dollars are as great a boon and relief as a few hundred would have been to me in my poverty. I did not know how much happiness I was going to get out of it."

I think this is a good place to stop, for all of us were happy in the thought that my dear mother's laborious life as the head of a large school was to end so happily, and that she would be able to rest and have time for the reading she so loved, and return to the country life which had become second nature to her, though conditions were so greatly changed, and she would certainly not have to complain of too many servants. I hope I have drawn her portrait and that of my father clearly enough for their children's grandchildren and great-grandchildren to form some idea of their characters. It is with that hope and desire I have drawn this imperfect sketch, and I will be perfectly repaid for my efforts if I succeed in interesting them in the past.

CHAPTER XXXIII

DADDY ANCRUM'S STORY

I ASKED Daddy Ancrum to come some day and tell me all he could remember about the past, and this morning while I was reading the lessons to Clarinda in the front piazza we saw him coming through the gate, dressed in his Sunday clothes, with a very clean white shirt and a rather battered derby, but worn with such an air that you knew it was superfine and not worn every day. I wish I had a picture of the old man; seems to me he has such a lovely face in his old age; his figure is now bent, but up to a few years ago it was very erect and powerful. Old as he is, he gives me a better day's work than any of the young ones. This is what he told me:

My mudder and fader was Ancrum and Henny, bought from Mr. Withers after de storm. The creditor come in and we haf fu sell. My ma tell me I ben five year old the March after the big storm. Maussa was a big man, he was just as supple, why maussa stan' too fine. When he walk in Georgetown every man and woman had

to look 'pon hum. When I cum to Georgetown
dere was only two full selling stores in town. All
was big house for lib in. When dem bring we to
town for sell, dem put up all de fambly, my uncle,
my aunty, my pa, my ma, and der cousin all together. Ole Mister Ben Allston come up to
maussa and trow 'e arm round maussa neck, and
he say: "Robert, step forward, the old Indigo
Bank ain't bruk yet." Den maussa gon up and
'e buy we all; Mr. Waterman want to buy me for
mek pilot on de sea, and he offer one tousand
dolla, but maussa woodn' let him have me. Ole
maussa used to live in dat little house you got for
study house. Maussa used to have all we chillun
cum to de house and bring a shell and fill um
with molasses, and we chillun ben dat happy and
play round and maussa ben in de piazza and drop
sleep, and we chillun lauf and say: "Luk a' buckra
de sleep." De fust chile I min' ben Clanda Ma
Maria. When I tak dat chile fu nurse ober ribber I see maussa been dat supple dat I seen him
myself jump across dat kenel. Den he choose me
to send me up to Marion to old Uncle Joe, 'bout
two miles from Warhee. I ben dey when maussa
married and de nex' yeah, when he gwine to de
mounting, him gone trough day for see de place,

[350]

and when he bring miss and Mas' Ben just been
ole nuff fu miss to travel, and Amy ben a nussing,
Maum Milly and Da Jeam's sister. Uncle Joe
send me fu bring de colt out de field and I bring
dem up so miss can see dem. Uncle Joe pint to
me and he say: "Robert, that's a smart boy.
Please God you must take good care of him."
Den maussa laff and say "Yes." Dem eat dinner
under de wagon shed an de two sarvan, Amy the
nuss and Hynes dribe de wagon, de Josey wagon,
and maussa dribe de carriage. No, didn't ben a
carriage, ben a baruche, wid de top tun back.
Dem gon on after dinner — den I nebber seen
miss or maussa till I hear say de place in Marion
sell to Mr. Tommy Godbald. Maussa had a hundred head of cattle and Mauma Milly mild 30
head ebery year and send down butter to miss
and ebery year Uncle Joe drive from 60 to 100
head o' hog. Dem had 500 acre of wild land —
Oh, my Lawd, if you wanna see plum you must
go dey, an' apple an' peach an' walnut an' ebery-
ting to eat. Bob been a big young man, an Peter
and Sampson and David, dem ben an' outlan'
people Afrikan, one ben Gullah and one ben a
Guinea — the Gullah ben a cruel people — and de
Fullah ben a cruel people, but Guinea ben a tough

[351]

workin' people, an' Milly ben a Guinea, milk de
cow, mak de butta, and bile and scald — and ma
Laud, you could pick up hominy off de flo'.
Now, after mauss sol' de place and all de cattle
an' hog, 'e only fech down de pepple and de hoss.
When we come down him ben on de beach and he
had annoder son name Robert. Him ben a longer
jinted boy, him was a pretty boy, an' I seen him
grown till he had on long ap'un. Maussa say
when I come hom I mus'n't stop on de plantation
dat night, I must go right over to the sheashore,
but de day I come an' Mary ben jus' out of him
time wid Billy, and him was to go down at dat
time back to de beach wid de baby, and dem had
to ge' befo' 'twas too late in de ebening, kase de
baby was so young. My business was to cut
marsh fo' de hoss and pick clam fo' de duck; dat
was at Kerneern an' I do dat an' Mary Grice was
de cook, te Amy ben de nuss, Uncle Hynes was de
coach driver, Moses Barren was de butler, Cæsar
was de hosler, Maum Ria was de seamster, an'
Lavina was de fine seamster, and a gal name
Cotter — an' Uncle Jeams Gallant was a fisher-
man — I met dem dere when I cum fus and Sandy
was de house boy, clean knife, rub mahogany, I
tell you we had someting to do den. Den Miss
Bly habe him sarvant ol' lady Mary Bly was 'e

right hand, Uncle Aleck was de coach driber, ol'
Uncle Stephen Bly ben de butler, but when him
come to stay wid miss, him fish principal kase de
was no wuck for him in de house. All dem supply cum from Friend-Field. Haklus was de cook,
when Miss Bly ben home, but now him had not'ing
to do but cut mash for de hoss, Miss Bly had t'ree
horse, Hope, Victory, and Active. Jack was de
tailor an' Fannie his wife was Miss Bly seamster,
Binna was de house gal, F'ederick was de boy go
behind de carriage, open gate an' ting. You ain't
know dat maussa own nearly all of Georgetown?
Dat Pint used to plant in corn and dat place make
all 'e own provision. I sell too much grass out o'
dat place. Mauss used to rule de whole shubang
— gracious Lord, Miss Bessie, when I study an'
look back and ting — an' fin' out — you say you
ben so po' I kyant believe, kase ole maussa ben
too rich — I know befoh de death of my ole
maussa, he put on de pole boat 50 jimmy john o'
brandy an' gin an' rum foh tek up to Cheraw
Bridge and put dem in Mr. Coker in sto', and one
boat carry 160 barrel of rice an' one carry 140
barrel, an' dem barrel hol' 9 bushel an' you ken
pack 10 in 'em, not dem little kag you call rice-
barrel now.

Maussa see somet'ing in me I didn' see in myself, an' he hol' me bak all 'e cud, den after I ben
in de house, an' den he put me in de field for a
while, and den he pint me to plow, an' den when
he put Peter in de field for ditch, an' den 'e pint
me to wait on Mr. Ellis. I wait on 'im about
seven years, but one summah maussa wen' travelling an' to de No'th, den Mr. Ellis treat me so
mean I run 'way an' lef' um. I done all 'e wuk
an' cut wood an' do eberything an' he pa cum
dere sick, an' when nite cum I hab to brush muskita off 'e pa, an' I brush de muskita as long as I
could keep awake, but I drop 'sleep and den Mr.
Ellis cum in and fin' me 'sleep, and take egvan-
tage o' me and beat me, an' den I clean up an'
lef', and I ben in de wood till I hear maussa cum
home. Den maussa didn' keep Mr. Ellis anoder
year, an' after dat I gone in de field an' after dat
he take me fo' plow-man ober ribber, an' after dat
on de high lan' — an' den 'e make me captain of
a gang in harvest, an' I was a regular arrand man,
I nebber wuck in de field no mo' — jes' tek cha'ge
of flat — carry supply to Waverly ebery week,
when maussa was gov'ner, carry down poultry,
vegetable, rice, butter to go down to miss in
Charlestown, bring back molasses, sugar, rum,

[354]

eberyt'ing, an' one time I was to take de house
sarvant to put on de boat to tek dem down to de
town, dem was to cum on de flat, 'bout middle
night, an' dem nebber cum till day clean, an' jus'
as dem come in, de boat gone. Nelson, William,
and Fibby — Fibby in de house, was ole Daddy
Thomas' daughta, and he ask maussa to buy her,
an' 'e bought her and two chillun, Nancy and
Jeams, an' afterwards she married Leander, the
mule tender. Cuffy was drowned swimming de
ribber with Buie, an' Sawney, too, dem had finish'
task soon, an' so dem start home an' swim de ribber, an' Cuffy had a bucket tie' round 'im neck
and 'e fill with water an' pull 'im down. I stan'
on de bank an' seen 'im drown. When I get to
Squirrel Crick wid de flat and de boat gone, an' I
hab to tek dat flat down to town, and dat tek me
till after dinner, an' I didn't hab nuffin to eat
'cause I was only spectin' to go to de mout' of
Squirrel Crick, an' dat boat gone in to Waverly,
tek a load of rice, an' pass me on de way, an'
he gone into Keith field, an' tek a load of rice,
an' pass me on de way, and when I get to town
I ben mos' dead, I ben dat hongry, an' Fibby say
to de captain, very polite, "Captain, can' you gib
these men something to eat, dey is mos' dead."

Den de captain said: "Dinner is done, and there ain't nutting but plenty of meat"; an' he gib we plen'y of meat, an' Fibby put 'e han' in 'e pocket an 'e tek out a twenty-five cents, an' give we, an' he say you can each send a dozen eggs down to Charlestown sometime to me. An' we gone an' buy rice.

After de wah come on and de sea all blockage an' maussa send me in charge o' 22 han' to wuck on fortification. In June I was wuckin ober de ribber an' maussa sen' foh me, fust de Driver Richard was to tell me, but he didn't wan' me to go, and I didn't wan' to go, and I gone ober ribber 'gen in m' task — and Mr. Belflowers sen' foh me, an' after maussa cum an' see me ben a fight foh hoe out m' corn, den maussa tell me I ken tek dat day fu finish m' corn, den Paul say we mus' leave at twelve or we can' ketch de train.

Maussa tell me, 'e say: "Boy, you see nobody hurt my hands, you ask the name of the person in charge and let me know, and when you go any-where to work, you ask the captain to put you in a tent by yourself, with your own men, don't mix up with other people." Now maussa tell me dat t'ree time', an' "Boy," he say, "go to my yaad when you get to Charleston."

We ben dere a good while, an' one day maussa
cum in a bright kerrige, an' eberybody hurrah, an'
maussa cum to we an' 'e say: "Well, boy, how you
gettin' on?" An' I say: "Not well, maussa. I
los' one of me man, Pompey, an' de res' sick, an'
dis place don' 'gree wid dem." He say: "Well,
you can't go till your wuck dun." "My maussa,
dis wuck'll nebber done. We'll dun, but de wuck
won't dun, we's all sick."

Maussa say: "Well, boy, if dat so you ken leave
to-morrow. You meet me in Charlestown Monday; this is Saturday. Don't let any of the hands
go over to Charlestown until you go." Jackson,
Fibby's brother, wen' off, but I couldn't stop him.
Monday we was to walk to Charlestown, maussa
tell de cap'ain put dem cross de bridge, but he
didn' put we over till eleven o'clock, so maussa
had to put we on de mail train. When we get to
Salters he tell Sam to give we each four quart of
rice an' then Paul Bryan drive we in de wagon
four miles and maussa tol' us to take two days to
get home, bu' we cum righ' 'ome dat same nite.
I tell you him been a number one maussa dat.
Him'll nebber back down from a man in trouble.
He'll save you if you is to save! The night we
left the wuk, Mr. King was killed that day.

When we got home maussa send me to a place called Britton's Neck, dere 'e was clearing up land to plant. After dat maussa bring me down and put me in a flat, and I carry de rice from Waverly Mill to Kingstree. He sent Saundy fust, den maussa cum to Britton's Neck, an' tell me: "Boy, I want one flat from Nightingdale Hall, three from Chicora, and two from Guendalow, take all to Waverly, and all take turns an' load and then start together, and go up the Black River to Kingstree, to the double bridge."

You couldn't pole in Waccamaw, you had to row, an' you couldn't pole in Black River 'til you get to Mr. Green, Rockingham, then you ken fin' sum polin' bottom. Sawny flat maussa put 111 barrel and one week after maussa sen' me an' tell me to ketch Sawny, an' Sawny ben unload, an' Mr. Shaw tek de rice an' haul half a mile about to de depot an den de railroad tek dem. Was a good deal of bad weather, and dat way it tuk me two weeks — Nightingdale flat only make one trip, but de odder five flat tek rice from Waverly to Kingstree three years, an' after dat maussa had two boat build, an' send me an' Joe Washington in charge of dem. My wife Maggie was a healthy woman 'til she begin to breed, but after

that maussa put her to mind de sheep. Maussa
say he nebber had any one fu' mind sheep like
she. When she call to de sheep "Come back
here," dey just wheel right round; when I gone
on de boat up ribber, maussa say my wife is very
sick, she was at de pint of death; I was near
Cheraw — we wus aground three days, and we
couldn't go, and I pray, an' I pray, an' I pray,
dat night, 'cause I couldn't lef' de boat on de
road and de Lawd sen' a big rain dat night and
raise de ribber thirty feet, and we gone up an'
git out de load an' gone right back home. An'
maussa tell me I mus' put Maggie on de boat, to
go up, an' I must walk and drive up de sheep Mr.
George Jeams had bought from him. "An' you
must drive them up to him, and then you go on
to a place I bought with my own money, and I
got ninety-five fine, good, prime people up there
and I want you to take charge of the place —
those people can't make feed enough there to keep
them four months; now I want you to see if you
can make a crop up there." Den I say: "Maussa,
what can I do with my cow and calf; I kyant lef'
them." Him say: "Well, take them right along
with you." Den I say: "Maussa, I got ninety
sheep fu' carry, and my cow got a raging calf, an'

how can I tek them all along, on dat journey all by myself." Den maussa say: "You can take Michael with you, till you get to Lynch's Creek, where two men will meet you and take the sheep."

Well, I start from de farm and de sheep travel so slow, and so tired, I never gone no fadder dan Mr. Blank way to Union Church; I stay dere dat night, an' de next day I gone to Lynch's Creek, an' I wait dere, an no man nebber come for de sheep, an' I just gone on an' tek de sheep and cattle, and when de man cum for de sheep dey had to follow me about twenty miles, an' den I tu'n Michael back an' I mek time on, an' when I get to de place, maussa send me to take charge of Morven, an' I tek charge, an' fust I build a house for Maggie, when 'e come, and I ben dere three week before Maggie cum. She had Pattie, and Kissie, and Pauline, and Aham; an' Peter, an' Peter Sweet's Louisa was on de boat, in delicate state, an' Maggie had to put dem to bed on de boat. An' when I ben dere one month maussa come, an' I been a clear ground when he come — he call fo' me and Mr. Yates, the agent, and Mr. Balentine, the obershear; Mr. Yates sit near de fire, wid maussa, I stand behind, and maussa say: "Well, Anchum, I bring you here to try and make a crop for me, and Mr. Balentine, I want you to put everything in his charge — he is to order the work, and he is to do the punishment, and I want you to put the keys in his hands too."

An' den I say: "Maussa, I well onderstan' de wuck, an' I'll tek charge of dat, but I don't want to tek no key." An' maussa say I must. But when maussa gone, I slip de key back in Mr. Balentine's hand an' say, "I don' want de key, you keep de key," an' maussa say to me: "You feed my horse and you feed Mr. Balentine's horse too, and your daughter Patty milk the cow." But I wouldn't let Patty milk, 'cause I wouldn't run 'cross Amy, him been a'milk, and I know what was going on, an' I knows dem people been eat de meat out o' de smoke-house, an' I know dem would tu'n it on me — so I wait till we fin' out, an' Mr. Balentine gib dat man, Chance Grate, an' he an' Abram Hynes an' himself were partners, and when Chance tuk some one else in the smoke-house without tell Abram he get mad an' tu'n State evidence an' tell me, an' I must ask Mr. Balentine: "Y' miss any meat?" An' he say "No." An I say: "Dat strange, 'cause Chance has got some; you'd better look." An' he gone in de smoke-house, an' miss a lot. He had kill an' cure fifty hog, and the meat ought to ben dere. When Mr. Balentine gone to count de meat he find half gone, den he gone with me to Chance house, an' dere he find two hams an' a shoulder, an' Mr. Balentine give him a big licking, 'til he confess how he done it. Den I stop him, I hold 'e hand an' I say: "Maussa only want de trut; he don't allow lick after dat, not another cut." Dere was two rice-barrel pack wid 300 bottle of ole wine in de cellar at Morven. I wucked and wucked and made a fine crop of peas, corn, and potatoes. Mr. Evans come up with ole miss to look at de crop, w'en I let her know I had housed de corn, one passel was shucked clean, an' Mista Evans, when he look at it, estimate 1,000 bushel of corn. Howsumeber, in de fall in February we hear de Yankees was bombarding Chiraw; eberybody was trying to get away from dat side, as de bridge was burned by we people. Two soldiers cum one nite an' ask me to let them spend de night — dey was what de people call de "Georgia Wild Cat." Dey say: "Ole man, de Yankees will be here before nine to-morrow morning." Dey hadn't sooner gone away from de house next morning, when de whole place was surround wid soldier, and dey call on de men to surrender.

[362]

What dey call de picket guard cum fust, and ax dat Daddy Hammedy fo' de key, an' when him hesitate, dem say, "I don't want no key," an' he just rushed up and kicked de door in, an' rushed in, and run up-stairs, and cum down with a bag full of silver, an' forks and spoons an' plate an' dat man say: "Ole man, de man dat own dis place must be a hell of a rich man, he got such fine tings." An' I say: "Yes, sir, my master is a powerful rich man." Den de oders run in an' git more; den dey gone — den we tought dey was all gone, when on a sudden de whole place full of people, from every corner — dey seem to rise right out de ground; now dis was de infantry, an' dey cum to station dere, and dey station dere for one week. Dem people just run dat grits-mill from de time day cum; dey just grind all de corn we mek, an' in a half hour de smoke-house was empty, and dey kill and dey fetch in, and dey kill and dey fetch in, and dey kill and dey fetch in, an' I got tired of it, I was sassy to them; I was wore out. Me an' Hammedy was de only man on de place; I jus' had to stey by de captain to perteck me and dese womens — den he put a guard an' tell dem to shoot any soldier dat went to burn or trouble de people. By de time dey was gone dere was nothing left but de rough rice — 400 bushels — an' dey couldn't manage dat; dey took all de corn, and if it hadn't been for de rice we would have starved. The Yankees left on Tuesday, an' de next Sunday Mr. Yates sent me word, I must take de people an' left at once; we must take de road, man, woman, and chillun; we must be gone Monday night — that I must take de hands and march off at once. I send George Green to tell miss, say "Come at once," and Tuesday miss cum, Daddy Eleck drive 'um, and Miss Bessie cum wid um, an' Mista Evans ride 'long side, an' miss say "What's matter?" an' I say: "Mr. Yates drive we, say we must lef'." Then miss say, "Well, turn to work, repair de land and plant what you can"; but I say: "Miss, I want to go home." Miss laugh and say: "Where is your home, Acrum?" I say: "Wherever you is, miss, dere is my home." An' miss say: "Well, if you go home now, 'tis too late to plant crop, so you had better plant your crop here, so by fall you can go after you gather the crop." So we done so, an' we mek a fine crop of corn and peas, an' when de time cum for to move, all de people what didn't have chillun tek dey fut an' gone, an' we big fambly couldn't do dat, an' I study, an' I study an' at las' I say to Daddy Hammedy: "You an' your son is carpenter, and you can mek a flat; I can tek a man an' cut down some big dead pine, an' haul dem in, an' we got saw-mill, and we can mek flat, and so we done, an' in two weeks after we done gather in de crop we had de flat done and ready to start on a Saturday; den we say we will move next week, and de people say let's go now, and so we done, but de oxen and ting worry me. Ole miss had send Mr. Yates and Mr. Balentine away an' got a young man name John Shaw in charge, and he done just what I say. Den I puswade March — he had a ole horse he pic' up — to tek de oxen down to ole miss to Society Hill, wid de hoss, and he done so. We started Sunday evening at four o'clock, and we did not get down to Chicora until de next Sunday night in de night. Me and Daddy Hammedy, an' his wife Mary Ann, an' my wife Maggie, an' his daughter Tyra, an' granddaughter Cherry, my chillun — Patty, Elizabeth, Pauline, Kizzie, Aham, and the baby Kilpatrick, then York Blye and Mary, his wife, and Joseph, Betsy, March's wife, Leah, and Hetty, and Flora, Phenix, and his wife Elizabeth, and his daughter Mary, and his daughter Miley, and Lucy. When I got off to

Chicora everything been tear up, people don gone crazy; now, when I left my house maussa tell me no one was to stay in my house till I come. I come back and find Moses in my house. I gone right in an' mek Moses come right out. Now Mauss Ben he done puty by me; I had nine head to feed, an' Mauss Ben say he feed them all fo' my wuck, so Mauss Ben feed my family fu' dat year, and feed dem well, an' we mek fine crop o' rice. The fust contract was you fu'nish land and seed and animals an' get two-thirds; I fu'nish wuck and get one-third. Every day I didn't wuck was deduct' from my share.

Daddy Ancrum advised a change to one-half, the hands to furnish the work animals as well as their own work, and the owner furnish the land in good fix, and seed rice, and it was divided equally in half. (This proved very successful, as they had their own work animals.)

INDEX

(Prepared by William B. Williford, 1976)

Abbeville, 44, 48, 140

All Saints' Church, Waccamaw, 101

Allston, Adèle, 86-87, 94, 96, 129, 132, 134-136, 139-140, 143-149, 164, 166-167, 171-172, 187-189, *passim*

Allston, Benjamin (father of R. F.W.), 3, 4, 55-56.

Allston, Benjamin (son of R. F. W.), 81, 84, 95, 147, 175, 269, 296, 342, 343, 366

Allston, Charles Petigru, 25-39, 114, 120, 126, 164-165, 221-223, 249, 271, 272, 275-280, 302-303, 308, 309, 331-333, 340, 342

Allston, Charlotte Ann (Mrs. Benjamin, mother of R. F. W.), 305

Allston, Charlotte Frances ("Fanny"), 75, 83-84, 94-95

Allston, Elizabeth Waties ("Bessie"), 75-76, 107-348

Allston, John (the Immigrant), 3

Allston, John (son of Immigrant), 3

Allston, John E., 344-348

Allston, Gen. Joseph, 33, 71

Allston, Joseph Blythe, 33-37, 71

Allston, Louise, 90, 91-92, 94, 95

Allston, Mrs. R. F. W. (née Adèle Petigru), 6, 43, 47-348

Allston, Robert Francis Withers, 4-39, 47, 57-137, 143, 175, 200-209, *passim*

Allston, William, 3, 17

Allston, William Allan, 33, 71

Allston, Washington, 83-84

Alston, Jane, 138-139

Alston, Rebecca, 138-139

Baruch (pron. *Bä-rook'*), Dr. Simon, 74

"Bel Rive" plantation, 158

Black River, 28-29, 157

Blythe, Mrs. Frances (Allston), 5, 75-80

"Brook Green" plantation, 56

"Canaan," Allstons' coastal home, 71-73, 99-100

Charleston, Allston family's home and social activities in, 141-142, 143-147, 163-166, 167-168, 187-189, 214, 298-306, 313-315, 320-333, 340-345

Cheves, Emma, 139

"Chicora Wood" plantation, 5, 8, 10, 11, 13-17, 21-22, 32, 36, 67, 72, 85, 123, 150-156, 202-209, 216-217, 252, 262, 267-269, 342-343

Christmas observance, 150-156

Civil War, 173-175, 183-184, 189-191, 218-248

Columbia, 24, 171, 176, 177, 237

"Crowley Hill," refuge in Darlington Co., 189, 192-202, 211-212, 218-238, 247-255, 313

Davis, Jefferson (Pres., CSA), 31, 175

"Ditchfield" ("Litchfield"?) plantation, 10, 209

Emerson, Dr. Isaac, 17

"Exchange" plantation, 8

"Friendfield" plantation, 74

[367]

INDEX

Georgetown, 4, 6, 35, 86, 173, 201, 207, 258, 261, 277-278, 296

Gibert (pron. *Zhe-bare'*), family, 43-46

Glennie, the Rev. Alexander, 101, 291

"Greenfield" plantation, 157

"Guendalos" plantation, 11, 209, 269-275

Hampton, Gen. Wade, 34, 38, 225

"Hasty Point" plantation, 158

Heyward, Annie, 300, 303

Huger (pron. *U-gee'*), Mr. and Mrs. Cleland, *163*, 165

Izard (pron. *Ih'-zurd*), Mr. and Mrs. Ralph, 157

LaBruce, Josh, 204

LaBruce, Kate, 139

Lee, Gen. Robert E., 147

Lesesne (pron. *Lĕ-sayne'*), Hal, 183

Lesesne, Henry D., 47, 84, 209, 210, 333-335

Lesesne, Mr. and Mrs. David, 333, 336-337, 338

"Loch Adèle," Allston farm in N. C., 213-216, 239, 242-247

Manigault, Joseph, 304-305

"Meadows, The," Allston summer house, 85-88, 96-99

Middleton, Oliver, 163

Nesbitt, Ruth, 182-183

"Nightingale Hall" plantation, 11, 210, 264-267

Pawley's Island, 11, 26, 67, 69-71, 100, 107, 111, 123, 137-138

Pee Dee River, 37, 68, 85, 88, 157, 158, 256, 317

Petigru-Pettigrew family, 46-59

Petigru, Adèle (later Mrs. R. F. W. Allston, *q.v.*), 6, 43, 47

Petigru, Ann (Mrs. Tom), 9, 10, 173

Petigru, Charles (USA), 47, 101-104

Petigru, James L., 5, 6, 10, 46, 47-48, 57, 84, 257, 298

Petigru, Mrs. James L., 57, 298-302

Petigru, Tom (Capt., USN), 47, 171

Pettigrew, Gen. J. Johnston (CSA), 174-175, 218

"Pipe Down" plantation, 9, 10, 11

Plantersville, 255, 261, 278, 283

Porcher, (pron. *Pô-shay'*) Marianna, 307

Porcher, Dr. Peter, 161

Porcher, Phil (Capt., CSA), 219-220

Porcher, Philip J., 47

Prince Frederick's Church, 34, 207, 208-209

Prince George's Church, 37

Pringle, Mrs. John Julius (née Izard), 156

Pringle, John Julius, 3rd., 176-177, 196, 225-226, 252-259, 276, 278, 290, 291-293, 332-333

Pringle, Mr. and Mrs. Julius Izard, 157, 255-264, 287-288, 294-295

Pringle, Mary, 176, 255, 262-264, 287, 316

Pringle, Poinsett, 190-191, 255, 256

"Prospect Hill" plantation (now part of "Arcadia"), 17

Poinsett, Mr. and Mrs. Joel, 156-157, 256

Poinsettia, introduction and naming of, 156

Ravene, Caro, 343

Read, Mr. and Mrs. J. Harleston, 158

Rice planting, 14-17, 67, 89-90

Sandy Island, 9

Secession, 173-175

Slavery and slaves, 7-10, 13-16, 61-65, 158-159, 169-171, 208-209, 212, 214-215, 269-275

Society Hill, 31, 32, 33, 48n, 189, 195, 211, 331

St. Cecelia Society, 35, 146, 169, 326, 327, 328, 333

St. Michael's Church, 49, 60, 187

South Carolina Jockey Club, 35, 146

Togno, Madame, 125-135, 139-140, 176-182

Trapier (pron. *Tra-peer'*), the Rev. Richard S., 291

Tucker, Dr. Dan, 295

Tucker, John, 157-158

Tucker, the Doctors, 158

Van der Horst (pron. *Van Dross*), Arnoldus, 187, 194, 225

Van der Horst, Mrs. Arnoldus, 187-189, 194, 225, 231, 234, 235, 295

Van der Horst, Lewis, 188, 231

Waccamaw River, 9, 26, 37, 56, 71, 101, 158, 210

"Waterford" plantation, 11, 210

Waties, John, 74, 75

"Waverly" plantation, 71, 111-114

Weston, Mr. and Mrs. Francis, 157, 205, 253-255

"White House" plantation, 156-157, 255-259, 262-264

Williams, John, 189

Williams, Mary, 314, 316, 333

Williams, Nicholas, 192, 313

Williams, Serena, 313-314, 316, 333, 338-339

CPSIA information can be obtained at www.ICGtesting.com
Printed in the USA
LVOW10s1745160914

404335LV00001B/194/P